I0176993

ABC's of Sewing
for the 4-H Club Girl

By Edna M. Callahan and Edith Berry
Extension Specialists in Clothing, the Ohio State University

_____

Name of member

_____

Age

_____

Member's address

_____

Name of club

_____

Advisor's name

Cooperative Extension Work in Agriculture and Home Economics, State of Ohio
The Ohio State University and the U. S. Department of Agriculture, Cooperating
Extension Service—Department of 4-H Club Work—W. H. Palmer, State Club Leader

Contents

*For Information and Circulars See Your County
Extension Agent.*

4-H Clubs

•

THE PLEDGE

I pledge my head to clearer thinking, my heart to greater loyalty, my hands to larger service, my health to better living, for my club, my community, and my country.

△

NATIONAL 4-H CLUB GIRL'S SONG

"Dreaming"

My home must have a high tree
　　Above its open gate.
My home must have a garden
　　Where little dreamings wait,
My home must have a wide view
　　Of field and meadow fair,
Of distant hill, of open sky
　　With sunlight everywhere.
　　　　　　　—Buchanan-Parish

△

WHAT EACH 4-H CLUB DOES

Each club has some woman in the community who acts as advisor. This advisor helps each girl plan her project. She and the girls plan the business and play of the club. If a girl does not know what to do in her project, or is uncertain how to do it, she can go to the club advisor for guidance.

All the girls in the club and the advisor plan together what they will do at the meetings, discuss the good health rules, and decide what each girl can do about them this year, find out what the club can do for the community, and plan how to do it. Together they plan how they can take part in county 4-H meetings. Achievement meetings are held each year and the girls and advisors help to plan them, and take part in the programs.

Once each year, too, the club exhibits the work of all its members either at a club meeting, a community meeting, or with all the other clubs in the county.

For Girls 11 and 12 Years of Age.

You probably want to know just what you do and make in this 4-H Club project. Each girl gets or makes a sewing box or basket. Then she:

1. Makes three of the articles shown and explained in this circular.

2. Fills in that part of the circular called "What do you know about ...." following the description of the articles she makes, and also fills in pages 5, 7, 8, and 20-21.

3. Scores the three articles she has made, on page 19.

If you are going to sew, of course you want to learn how to sew correctly. Read pages 6 to 8 before you start to sew. Have you ever looked at the things made of fabrics which you use and wear every day? Some are made by hand and some by machine. You will want to sew that way too, so learn to sew with the sewing machine as well as by hand, and then learn to decide when it is best to do your work by hand and when by machine.

Helping select the material, pattern, and trimming for the articles you make is fun, and another thing each 4-H Club girl does. Of course you will want to talk this over with your mother, your advisor, and the other girls in the club.

You probably want to know how you can help make your 4-H Club one of the BEST. Here are some things to do:

1. Try to attend all meetings of the club, be on time, bring the article you are making, do your part on the program.

2. Attend as many county meetings as possible, and go on the trips and tours planned for your club. You will want to take part in the health program of your own club and do your share of its community services.

3. You may be asked to be a leader, an officer, or serve on committees. These are honors you will enjoy.

4. Finish your work. Make the articles, do the necessary writing to complete your circulars, exhibit your three articles, and help with the last judging of them and of your circulars.

PLANNING YOUR PROJECT WORK

Look at the pictures in this circular. Talk them over with your mother and advisor. Which of these do you need? Which ones can you make easily and neatly? If you have never used a sewing machine you may want to make a part or perhaps one whole article with it.

The first year you are in a clothing project you will want to have a pair of shears, pins, needles, and other sewing supplies in a basket or box you can call your own (see page 6).

After arranging a sewing box of your own, you will be ready to make the three articles which you, your mother, and advisor think you should make. You may make any three of the articles found in this circular:

Pincushion	Bean bag	Book cover
Needlebook	Hot pan holder	Dust cloth
		Tea towel

Write in the blanks the names of the articles you plan to make after you have your sewing box arranged.

1. .... 2. ....

3. ....

HINTS FOR THE CLUB GIRL

1. Keep your hands and nails clean.
2. Wear a clean dress when sewing. It will help keep your work clean.
3. Sit with back straight, feet flat on the floor, and in a good light.
4. Place your sewing on a table, not in your lap, while working.
5. Always cut thread with shears or scissors. Do not break or bite it.
6. Use a short thread, about 24 inches long.
7. Always wear and use a thimble when sewing.
8. When cutting, hold shears with the narrow blade down.
9. To cut a straight edge, pull a thread of the fabric and cut along this thread (see page 22).
10. Read and follow directions carefully.
11. Always do your work the best you can.
12. Do all your own work. Ask others for advice only.

CHECKING UP ON YOURSELF

After you make each article, answer these questions with "yes" or "no."

Did you always:	1st Article	2d Article	3d Article
1. Wash your hands before beginning to sew?....			
2. Sit with your back straight and feet flat on floor?			
3. Keep your sewing on a table while sewing?....			
4. Cut threads with scissors?.....................			
5. Use a thimble when sewing?.................			
6. Hold shears, narrow blade down when cutting?			
7. Pull a thread of fabric, to cut a straight edge?...			
8. Do your work the best you could?...........			
9. Do all the sewing youself?...................			

A good workman always has good tools in his tool box. 4-H sewing club members need some tools also, and a box or basket in which to keep them. To pick up a workbox and know that all the supplies you need are in it, makes sewing easier and more fun.

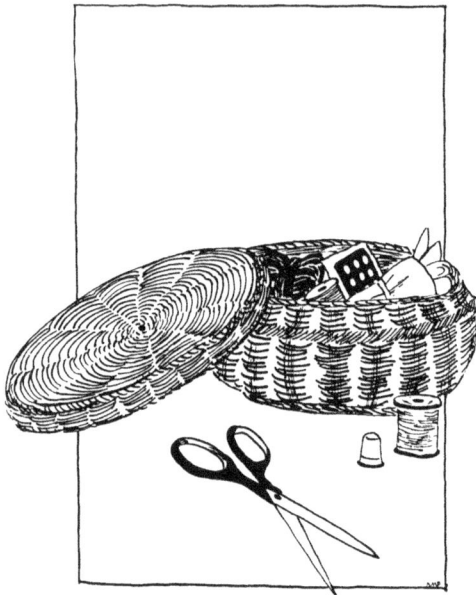

Small baskets and boxes make good workboxes (Fig. 1). Tin marshmallow cans, cake boxes, flat coffee cans, or candy boxes may be used. These may be painted on the outside and lined on the inside with a gay print or plain fabric.

Special pockets for thread, thimble, tape measure, scissors, emery, and other small articles may be sewed to the lining. Several long, thin nails may be driven into the bottom of wooden boxes or into a thin, narrow piece of wood cut to fit in a tin box. The nails may be used as racks for spools of thread.

Fig. 1.—Attractive sewing basket.

After the first club meeting, you will want to find or make a pretty box and put in it the few supplies you will need for sewing. Take your workbox to the second club meeting. Your advisor and the other 4-H Club members will like to see what a pretty and useful box you have made.

Your Sewing Supplies

Sewing tools needed are: needles, emery bag, thread, pins, thimble, shears, tape measure, pincushion, notebook, pencil, and a box to hold these articles.

Needles.—A good sewing needle is slender, so that it will push through the fabric easily. A long eye is easily and quickly threaded. Needles numbering 7 to 9 are a good size for hand sewing.

Emery Bag.—An emery bag is used to make needles smooth if they rust or become sticky. Needles should not be kept in it, because the emery rusts them in time.

Thread.—Cotton thread is numbered from 8 to 200. The higher the number the finer the thread. Nos. 60 to 70 are used for most hand and machine sewing. Select a size of thread to match the size of yarns in the fabric to be sewed. Then the stitches, if neatly made, will show little.

Pins. — Pins are used to hold two or more layers of fabric together or to mark a line. A sharp pointed, slender pin is easy to stick into fabric and leaves only small holes when taken out. A pin that has a "hook" on the point will pull the yarns of a fabric and spoil it. A good place to keep pins is in a pincushion.

Thimble. — A thimble keeps the eye of a needle from hurting the end of the finger as the needle is pushed through a fabric. It should fit the middle finger so that the tip of the finger rests against the top of the thimble. Light weight metal or celluloid thimbles are best.

Tape Measure. — A tape measure or ruler is needed for measuring. A tape measure should be made of firm material, with metal tips on each end, and the numbers should be plainly marked.

Measuring Gage. — Light weight cardboard may be notched to make a guide for measuring the width of seams, hems, bindings, etc.

Scissors. — Scissors with sharp, smooth blades are needed for straight, even cutting. They should be of a size that fits your hand.

Notebook and Pencil. — A notebook and pencil, kept in the sewing box, are handy for taking notes about your sewing.

Table. — You will need a table on which to work. It should be large enough to hold your fabric and sewing box. It should be of a height that is easy for you to work on when seated.

Pressing Equipment. — It is wise to press an article often while making it. Have a clean, warm iron and an ironing board close by when sewing.

MAKE A PLAN FOR YOUR SEWING BOX

Study pages 5 to 8, and fill in these blanks before you begin to make and arrange your sewing box.

1. Name three kinds of boxes which you might use for your sewing box. Check (√) the one you are using. a..
   b.. c...

2. List the supplies you think should be in a sewing box. Check (√) those you have in yours.

....

....

....

3. Fill in each of these blanks with a word that will make each sentence true.

   a. A good sewing needle is .... enough to push through the fabric easily.

   b. A needle with a .... eye is more easily threaded than one with a small eye.

   c. Select a size of thread to match the size of .... in the fabric.

   d. A.................... pointed .... pin is easy to stick into fabric.

   e. For straight, even cutting, scissors should have .... edges.

   f. Rust may be removed from a needle by sticking it through an ....

7

What young girl does not long to use a sewing machine before her mother thinks she is old enough? After girls learn to use it, what fun they have making things which they could not make as well by hand!

All sewing machines are much the same. Every girl who uses a sewing machine should know the parts of that machine, what these parts do, and how to care for the machine. Read the book of directions that comes with the machine, or have someone teach you how to use the machine.

The upper and lower tensions on the machine should be turned so that a firm smooth stitch is made. Machine stitching should look like A in Fig. 3. Learn to make straight, even rows of stitching. If stitching is done along an edge it should be as close to the edge as it is possible to stitch.

When using a sewing machine, there are some things to keep in mind. Study these before you try to use a sewing machine:

1. Sit well back in the chair. Keep your back straight but lean body forward a little.
2. Place both feet on the treadle of the machine.
3. Try the machine stitch to be sure it is neither too short nor too long to be strong, and look pretty.
4. Be sure the upper or lower thread of the machine stitch is neither too tight nor too loose. If upper thread lies flat on the fabric the upper tension is tighter than the lower. If the lower thread lies straight on the fabric, the lower tension is tighter than the upper (see Fig. 3).
5. Stitch straight and evenly.
6. Raise the needle and take-up lever when stitching is done, then raise presser foot, and pull work toward back of machine.
7. Cut thread, using cutting blade on machine or scissors.

Fig. 2.—How should you sit at the sewing machine?

What Do You Know About Sewing Machines?

1. Did you use a sewing machine to make any of your articles? ....

2. Check (√) the picture in Fig. 2 you think shows a good position at the sewing machine.

3. When you are ready to do your first sewing machine stitching, check your sewing machine stitch by stitching on a piece of cloth. Your sample may look like one of the three stitches shown here.

a. Does your sample look like A, B, or C? Fig. 3.

b. If your sample looks like B or C what will you need to do to either the upper or lower tensions to make the sample look like A? ....

....

A—Both tensions correct

B—Upper tension tighter than the lower.

C—Lower tension tighter than the upper.
—Copyright, S. M. C.

Fig. 3.—Machine stitching.

Making Your Articles

•

PINCUSHION

Every girl who sews needs her own pincushion. You may make one for your sewing box. A good pincushion is small, soft, and light in weight.

Materials — Cut two 5½ by 4-inch pieces of wool flannel or other soft wool fabric. This may be taken from an old dress, suit, or coat; or a scrap of new wool fabric may be used. A smooth, plain colored fabric in a medium or dark color is best. Use a color that you like and one that will look pretty in your sewing box. Find enough hair, wool, wool yarn, or scraps of wool fabric to stuff the cushion. Use thread to match the fabric.

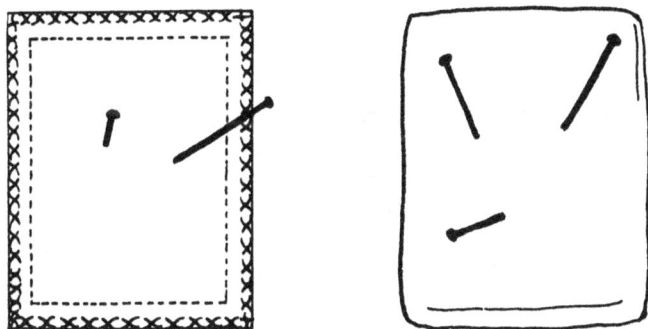

Fig. 4.—A handy place for pins.

Making the Pincushion. — There are a number of ways to make a pincushion (see Fig. 4). One way is to place the two pieces of fabric on top of each other and pink all edges with pinking shears or notch them by hand. Machine stitch ½ inch from the edges. Begin about the center of one side and stitch all the way around, ending about 2 inches from the starting place. This makes an opening for stuffing the cushion. Fasten ends of machine stitching by retracing (page 22), or by tying the threads tightly. Fill the pincushion with hair or wool and sew across the opening by machine, or by hand, using the back stitch (page 23).

Instead of pinking the edges, you may machine stitch ¼ inch from the raw edges, then blanket stitch over the edges (page 24) with colored yarn. Still another way is to make a plain seam (page 25), on the wrong side, leaving an open space for stuffing. Turn cushion right side out, stuff it, and slip stitch (page 25) the open edges together.

Any one of these make a good pincushion, but other shapes and kinds may be made.

I. Before you begin to cut and make your pincushion, plan what you will do first, second, third, etc., and write your plan in the following blanks.

1. ....   4. ....

2. ....   5. ....

3. ....   6. ....

II. After your pincushion is made, answer these questions:

1. What kind of fabric did you use for your pincushion? ....

2. What did you use for stuffing? ....

3. As you use it, does the size seem just right, too large,. or too small? ....

....

4. Do pins and needles stick into the cushion easily? ....

III. Score your pincushion, using the score card on page 19.

NEEDLE CASE

A needle case filled with different sizes of needles is easier to use than the paper package in which needles come when you buy them at the store. Needles may be kept in a pincushion when sewing, but if left there, they often get lost. A needle case makes a safe place to keep needles when not in use. The case may be any shape (see Fig. 5), but a small booklet is easy to make and use.

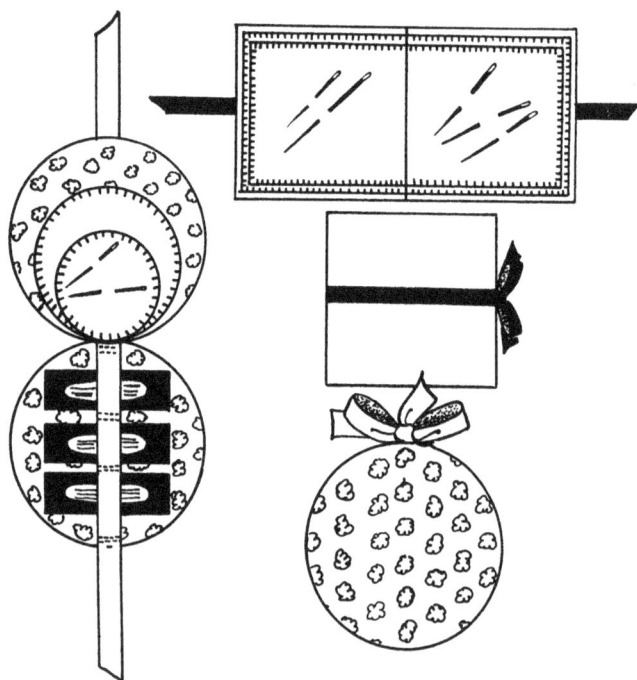

Fig. 5.—Needle case.

Material.—The outside cover may be made of flannel, crash, felt, oilcloth, percale, or gingham. A fabric with a small check or figure is better for this small article than a large printed fabric. Use a medium color, not too light, dark or bright. You may find a pretty piece of used fabric or a new scrap at home for your needle case. A good size for the cover is 3½ inches by 5 inches, or 4 inches by 6 inches. For the inside leaves, use one or two pieces of light weight plain colored flannel or other woolen fabric cut ½ inch smaller than the cover. About 12 inches of cord or ribbon is needed if the leaves and cover are tied together.

Making a Needle Case. — If cover is to be unlined, finish the edges by binding (page 26) or by hemming (page 25); or blanket stitch (page 24) over the raw edges. If you wish, the cover may be lined with silk or cotton fabric cut the same size as the cover. Place right sides together and baste. Then machine stitch the cover and lining close to the edge, except for about a 2-inch space. Turn seam to inside and slip-stitch (page 25) the open space together. Another way to join lining to cover is by blanket stitching (page 24) the raw edges of both together.

Finish the cut edges of the leaves by pinking them or with a blanket stitch (page 24). Fold the cover through the center to make a booklet. Fasten leaves to cover at center fold of booklet by machine stitching the layers of fabric together or by tying them with yarn cord or ribbon.

What Do You Know About Needle Case?

I. Before you begin to sew, plan the things you will do first, second, third, etc., in making your needle case and write your plan in the blanks:

1. ....   4. ....

2. ....   5. ....

3. ....   6. ....

II. You will need to answer these questions when planning a needle case. Do this before you begin to cut or sew.

1. What kind of fabric shall I use for a cover? ....

2. What color needle case will look best in my sewing basket? ....

3. What size shall I make the cover? ....

4. What kind of stitches shall I use in making the case? ....

.................., ..., ...

III. After you have made your needle case, answer these questions:

1. Is my needle case pretty? ....

2. Is it too small, too large, or a good size? ....

3. Do you find it a handy place to keep needles? ....

IV. Score your needle case, using the score card on page 19.

Any girl who enjoys books and takes pride in keeping them clean and new looking will like to make book covers.

Material — Any firm fabric such as percale, linen, crash, cretonne, ging-ham, denim, or oilcloth makes pretty and lasting book covers. Fabrics with small flowers, checks, or narrow stripes show dirt less than plain fabrics. Select pretty colors which are not too light, dark, or bright.

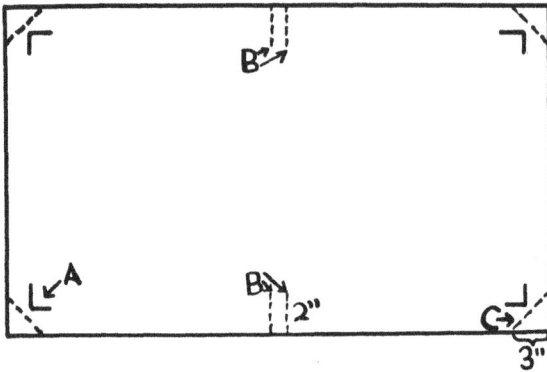

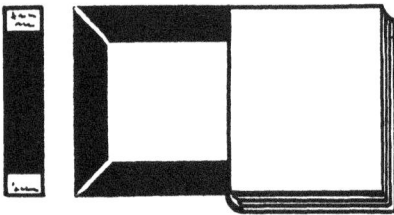

Making a Book Cover. — Wrap fabric around closed book, being sure that the threads of the fabric lie straight with the edges of the book. With pins mark on the fabric the four corners of the book as in Fig. 6A. Also mark curved end of book, Fig. 6B. Lay fabric out flat and cut the cover 2 inches beyond corner marks on all sides. Cut off each corner, beginning and ending about 3 inches from the corners, Fig. 6c, leaving ¼ inch for a seam. Slash from edge of fabric to marks B, showing place of curved end of book. Turn these narrow strips of fabric toward center of cover, and to wrong side of fabric.

Fig. 6.—Making a book cover.

Fold cut edges at corners together creasing on corner markings. Stitch about ¼ inch from cut edges. This miters the corners. Press seams flat and turn cover right-side out. Overcast, page 24, all raw edges.

What Do You Know About Book Covers?

I. Before you start to make a book cover, plan how you will make it. To do this you will need to answer these questions. Fill in the blanks.

1. Three good fabrics for book covers are ...., ..., and ....

2. Shall I use a plain color fabric, a small print or a large printed fabric? ....

3. What color will please me most and look best in my room? ....

4. Will the fabric I am using wash well and not fade? ....

II. Before beginning to make the cover, plan what you will do first, second, third, etc., and write your plan in the following blanks.

1. ....   4. ....

2. ....   5. ....

3. ....   6. ....

III. After you have made your book cover answer these questions about it:

1. Does the cover fit the book tightly? ....

2. Is the color pretty? ....

3. What kind of fabric did you use? ....

4. Does this fabric make a firm book cover? ....

IV. Score your book cover, using the score card on page 19.

BEAN BAG

What fun may be had with bean bags! The whole family likes to play with them. This is a fine chance for club girls to work with bright colors, for bean bags may be gay, as well as pretty in shape and color.

Material. — A bean bag should be of a size which will handle easily — a 6-inch square makes a good size bean bag. The fabric should be strong and firmly woven. Use a fabric such as gingham, denim, heavy muslin, ticking or toweling. You may find in your home enough fabric of the right kind out of which to make a bean bag. A fabric of medium color will show dirt less than light or dark colors. Checks and small figured fabrics look clean longer than plain colors. Bright colors make pretty bean bags, but be sure the colors you use are pretty together. A bean bag of red and white checked gingham bound with plain red bias binding may be much prettier than a green and orange print fabric bound with red binding.

Making a Bean Bag. — Square, round, or an odd shape may be used for a bean bag. To make a square bean bag, cut two pieces of fabric about 6¾ inches square. Lay right sides of pieces together. Pin at each corner and between the corners. Baste (page 22) ⅜ inch from the cut edges on the four sides.

Begin machine stitching 1 inch from one corner, stitch ½ inch toward next corner. Retrace (see page 22) and stitch around the square, using the basting as a guide. Stitch 1 inch past the fourth corner, turn and retrace (page 22), to fasten thread.

Turn the bag inside out through the opening left in the stitching. Fold and baste each side of the opening to the wrong side the width of the seam. Press the bean bag with warm iron. Fill bag a little more than half full of beans. Bring the sides of the opening together and overhand (page 23), or slip stitch (page 25) them closely.

Here is another way of making bean bags. With wrong sides together, baste around the square of fabric, using very short basting stitches (page 22).

Before basting the last 2 inches, fill bag half full of beans. Baste across 2-inch opening. The raw edges may be bound with bias binding to match the main color in the fabric. See page 26, to learn how to join bias binding and how to sew binding to fabric.

What Do You Know About Bean Bags?

I. Before making a bean bag, answer these questions:

   1. Name three things to keep in mind when selecting fabric for a bean bag.

         ...., ...

     and ....

   2. Name four kinds of fabric suitable for bean bags. Check (√) the one you plan to use.

       a. ....   c. ....

       b. ....   d. ....

   3. Plan the things you will do first, second, third, etc., to make your bean bag, and write your plans in the following blanks.

       a. ....   d. ....

       b. ....   e. ....

       c. ....   f. ....

II. After you have finished your bean bag, answer these questions:

   1. How full did you fill the bag with beans? ....

   2. Is the bean bag easy to throw and catch? ....

   3. Did you use any trimming on the bag? .... If so, what kind? ....

III. Score your bean bag, using score card on page 19.

HOT PAN HOLDER

So many kitchens do not have enough hot pan holders (see Fig. 7). Tea towels should not be used for this purpose because there is danger of a long cloth catching fire. Neither is a tea towel easy to handle nor thick enough to keep the hands from being burned.

Club girls like to check up on the number of holders their mothers, aunts, and friends have, and make them a good supply. It is a good plan to have at least four holders so that two may be in use while the other pair is in the laundry.

Materials. — A good size for the outer covers is 7 inches square. Gingham, percale, or other washable fabric may be used. White and dark colors show soil more than medium colors. Checked and printed material show soil less than plain fabrics. Pretty holders may be made of colors used in the kitchen. They may match the color of the walls, tea towels, aprons, or be made of another color which is pretty with the other colors in the kitchen.

For the lining cut two squares ½ inch smaller than the cover. These may be of outing flannel, or pieces of an old clean blanket. Cut a loop for hanging up the holder. It may be of narrow woven tape, a strip of fabric like the holder, or ready made bias binding the same as the edge of the holder is bound with. A small wire or bone ring may be sewed to one corner, instead of the loop.

Making a Hot Pan Holder. — Turn edges of each square of fabric about ⅜ inch to the wrong side. Crease and baste near the fold. Place one square on the table with wrong side up. Lay the padding or lining fabric over this square. Pin and baste together. Place second square on top, right side of fabric turned upward. Baste this square in place, keeping corners and edges even.

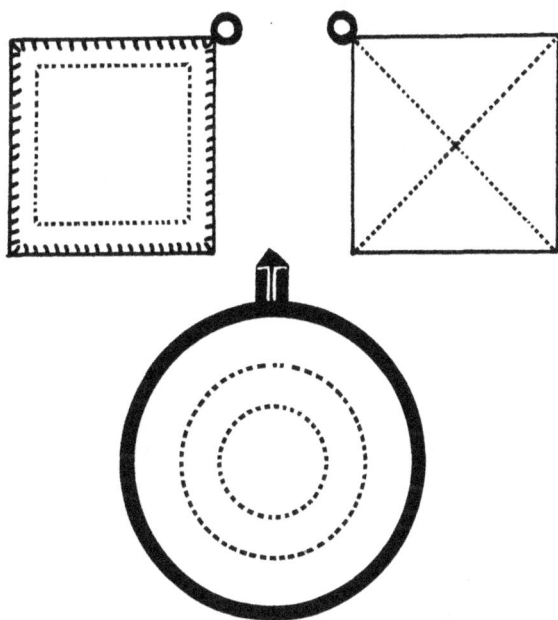

Fig. 7.—Hot pan holders, round and square.

Make a loop of a 4-inch piece of narrow woven tape, or cut a strip of the fabric 1 inch wide and 4 inches long. Fold lengthwise through the center, crease raw edges to inside, and machine stitch or slip-stitch (page 25) the folded edges together.

To fasten loop to holder, slip one end of loop ½ inch under upper square of fabric on one side of a corner. Slip other end of loop under square on one side of corner.

Machine stitch around the holders, stitching close to the edge. Stitch across the pad from corner to corner to hold padding in place. Fasten the threads by retracing (page 22) or by tying the ends tightly.

The edges of the holder may be blanket stitched (page 24) or overhanded (page 23) together instead of machine stitched. If blanket stitched, use a cotton yarn of a color that matches or blends with the color of the fabric. Use No. 60 or 70 sewing thread for overhanding.

Still another way of holding the layers of fabric together is by binding them with bias binding (page 26). Stitch bias loop along edge and slip ends of loop under edge of binding before machine stitching binding to holder.

What Do You Know About Pan Holders?

I. Before making a hot pan holder, plan the kind of holder you would like to have by answering the following questions:

   1. What size should a hot pan holder be? ....

   2. Name two good shapes for a holder ....

   3. What color or colors will look best in the kitchen for which you are planning a pan holder? ....

   4. What stitches will you need to know and use? ....,
........................, ...

II. The following sentences are not finished. Place words in the blanks that will make the sentences true.

   1. Hot pan holders may be made of ...., ... or other washable fabrics.

   2. Hot pan holders may be lined with .... or ....

   3. The edges of a holder may be finished by........................, ... or ....

   4. To hang up a hot pan holder when not in use, it should have a loop made of .... or ....

III. Before you begin to cut and sew your hot pan holder, plan the things you will do first, second, third, etc., and write your plan in the following blanks.

   1. ....   3. ....

   2. ....   4. ....

IV. After you have made a hot pan holder try it out and answer these questions:

   1. It is of a size that is easy to handle when lifting a hot pan? ....

   2. Is it thick enough to keep your hand from being burned? ....

   3. Is the loop long enough and so placed that it can be easily slipped over a nail? ....

   4. Does the color of the holder blend with other colors in the kitchen? ....

V. Score your hot pan holder, using the score card on page 19.

DUST CLOTH

Dusting is more fun if one has a pretty dust cloth to use. Girls like to keep clean dust cloths in their own rooms where they will be handy.

Material. — Cheesecloth and soft unbleached muslin make dust cloths which will not scratch the furniture and will take up dust easily. Select a loosely woven muslin because it is soft, or a firm quality of cheesecloth because it is easier to hem and will last longer than a thin, loose quality. Cut a square or rectangle. This may be about 24 inches square, or 24 by 30 inches.

Making a Dust Cloth. — Baste a ¼- to ½-inch hem all around the dust cloth, turning square corners. If the fabric is of a firm quality stitch close to the edge with a sewing machine, using thread the color of the cloth. Instead of stitching on the sewing machine, the hems may be put in with small running stitches, made with one or two strands of colored cotton thread.

What Do You Know About Dust Cloths?

I. Before making your dust cloths plan the kind you would like to make by answering these questions:

   1. Why should dust cloths be made of soft material? ....

   2. What two shapes are best for dust cloths? .... and ....

   3. How wide will you make the hem around your dust cloth? ....

   4. Is the cheesecloth you are using firm in quality or quite loose and thin? .... Is the muslin soft? ....

   5. Will you hem it by hand or machine? ....

II. Plan the things you will do first, second, third, etc., in making your dust cloth and write your plan in the following blanks.

   1. ....   4. ....

   2. ....   5. ....

   3. ....   6. ....

III. After you have made your dust cloth try it out and answer these questions:

   1. Does it scratch polished furniture? ....

   2. Does it leave lint on dark furniture? ....

   3. Is it too large to hold easily in your hand? ....

   4. Is it too small to take up the dust quickly? ....

IV. Score your dust cloth on the score card, page 19.

TEA TOWELS

Every kitchen needs many tea towels. They should take up water readily, and launder easily and quickly. Linen dries a wet surface quickly but some cotton towelings which have the starch washed out are quite easy to use. Feed or sugar sacks, which have all lettering washed out, may be used for towels. Embroidery is not needed on tea towels, and if it is used it should be quite simple, such as a row of cross or blanket stitches on the edge of the hem. Narrow well-made hems are just as pretty and are easy to iron (Fig. 8).

Material. — Towels are usually made

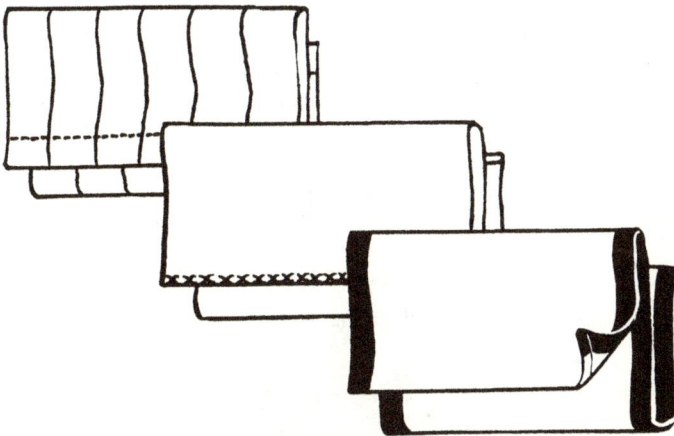

Fig. 8.—Tea towels.

of linen, cotton, or union toweling which is 18 inches long. Tea towels may be from 27 to 36 inches long. Some people like a long towel while others like a shorter one. Toweling cut 36 inches in length makes a good size towel after hems are turned.

Making a Towel. — Draw a thread of the material across each end of the towel and cut off the uneven ends along this thread. If a towel is cut from a feed sack, straighten (page 22) the longer sides in the same way.

Turn in the raw edges ¼ inch and crease again at the top of the raw edge, making a hem about ¼ inch. Pin and baste hem in place, matching stripes or checks of turned edge with those of the towel. The napery hem (page 26) may be used on linen towels. Towels of other fabrics may be hemmed with a small slanting hemming stitch (page 25), or sewed with the sewing machine close to edge of hem. Towels made of sacks should be hemmed along the sides as well as the ends. Overhang (page 23) the open ends of the hems together so no raw edges show. Take out bastings, press, and fold neatly.

What Do You Know About Towels?

I. Before making your towel, plan the kind you would like to make by answering these questions:

   1. What fabric takes up water most easily and quickly? ....

   2. What is a good length .... inches, and width .... inches for a tea towel?

   3. What kinds of stitches will you use to make your towels? .... ,

   .... , ... , ... , ...

II. These sentences are not finished. Place words in the blanks that will make the sentences true.

   1. Feed sacks which have .... washed out may be used for towels.

   2. Before making a towel, the ends of the fabric should be straightened by

   .... a thread and .... along this line.

III. Before beginning to work on your towel, plan the things you will do first, second, third, etc., in making it and write your plans in the blanks:

   1. ....   3. ....

   2. ....   4. ....

IV. After you have made your towel, try it out then answer these questions with "yes" or "no.".

   1. Does it take up water easily, and quickly? ....

   2. Does the fabric and color look well in the kitchen where it is to be used?

   ....

   3. Is it large enough or small enough to be easy to handle when drying dishes?

   ....

V. To learn how well you have made your towel, score it on the score card, page 19.

Scoring Your Articles

When scoring each article, ask yourself these questions: Will it wear well? Is it made in the right way? Does it look neat on both right and wrong sides?

Thinking of your answers, place a check mark ($\vee$) in column 4, 3, 2, or 1, across from each of the points you score.

To figure the value of the check marks, multiply the number of marks in each column by the figure at the top of the column. To get the final score, add the total values of the check marks and divide by the number of points scored.

4—A, Excellent   3—B, Good   2—C, Fair   1—D, Poor.

SCORE CARD

Name of Articles ☞												
POINTS TO SCORE	4	3	2	1	4	3	2	1	4	3	2	1
Suitable size and shape												
Suitable color or colors												
Suitable kind and quality of fabric												
Suitable kind of seams, hems, etc.												
Suitable kind of stitches												
Suitable kind and size of thread												
Width and evenness of seams												
Width and evenness of hems and bindings												
Size and evenness of hand stitches												
Ends of threads fastened tightly												
Other finishes, if any												
Is article clean, well pressed?												
Is article pleasing to look at?												
Total value of check marks												
Final Score (4, 3, 2, 1)												
Final Grade (A, B, C, D)												

How Much Have You Done?

When you became a 4-H Club member, you agreed to attend local club meetings; to serve as an officer; or if you did not, to serve on committees; to help the group plan the program for the club and to help to carry it out; to do your own project work and exhibit when your club exhibits.

How much have you done in your club? Put a check mark (√) after each item to which you can say "yes."

HAVE YOU SERVED —— Check (√)

As a leader? ....

As an officer? ....

On committees? ....
Write here the kind of committees on which you served:

....

....

....

....

DID YOU HELP PLAN THE LOCAL 4-H CLUB PROGRAM? Write what you did below:

....

....

....

....

....

....

....

HAVE YOU ATTENDED —— Check (√)
County meetings, tours, trips, camp achievement day?... ....
Write below the events you attended:

....

....

....

....

DID YOUR CLUB DO ANY COMMUNITY SERVICE? (Write here what your club did)

....

....

....

....

....

DID YOUR CLUB HAVE A HEALTH PROGRAM? ——
Write here what your club did and what part you took.

....

....

....

....

....

DID YOUR CLUB TAKE PART IN ANY STATE MEETINGS?
Write here how your advisor or members took part.

....

....

....

....

....

When you started this project you agreed to arrange a sewing kit if you did not have one, or add to one you already own; to plan, make and score three articles; to fill in the blanks called your record, and to exhibit when your club exhibits.

How much did you do in your project?

After each question to which you can answer "yes" put a check mark (√).

DID YOU PLAN YOUR ARTICLES? ....

DID YOU HELP IN THE SELECTION OF FABRICS? ....

Did you make your three articles yourself? ....

Did you score your three articles? ....

Is your record all filled in on page 20? ....

Is your record all filled in on page 6 (planning your sewing box) and on page 8 (checking up on your sewing machine)? ....

Is your record filled in for the three articles you made?.... ....

Did you equip a sewing kit if you did not already have one? ....

Did you exhibit your three articles when your club exhibited? ....

Where did you exhibit?...... ....

....

How MUCH HAVE YOU LEARNED ——

Have you learned ——   Check (√)

How to use the sewing machine? ....

How to put colors together so they are attractive? ....

How to decorate articles suitably? ....

How to select fabric of good value? ....

Write here other things you have learned:

....

....

....

....

....

....

....

What can you do to improve or do your sewing better?

Write here what you think you can do to improve your articles:

....

....

....

....

To Make Stitches, Seams and Hems

•

To Cut a Straight Edge

Cut into the fabric about ½ inch. If there is a selvage, cut through the width of the selvage. Catch hold of a thread raveled from this cut edge. Pull thread carefully to pucker the fabric. This gives a straight line along which to cut. If thread breaks, pick up another thread along cut edge and pull it as a guide for cutting the edge straight.

Retracing to Fasten Machine Stitching

When beginning a line of stitching, stitch back from the direction in which you wish to sew, for a distance of ½ to 1 inch. With needle down in the fabric raise the presser foot of the machine. Turn fabric around and stitch over the few stitches just made and continue to end of stitching. When end of stitching is reached, raise presser foot, turn work around and sew back over line of stitching, for about an inch. Draw all ends of thread through to under side and cut off close to fabric. If sewing machine stitching goes entirely around an edge so that the ends meet as when stitching around a square or circle, begin stitching without retracing. Stitch around edge to starting point and overlap stitching for about 1 inch. Cut off threads.

Stitches

Basting Stitch

Place work flat on table and pin together the edges to be basted. Pins should be put in at right angles to edge.

Begin with a knot in the thread. Working from right to left, stick the needle in the fabric; bring it out again about ½ inch ahead, making a stitch straight with the edge. Draw the thread tight enough that it will be flat on the fabric. When basting is done, fasten thread by taking two or three small stitches one above the other. This makes the thread easy to rip out (see Fig. 9). Basting stitches are used to hold two or more layers of fabric together until machine stitched or sewed by hand.

Fig. 9.—Even basting.   Fig. 10.—Back stitch.

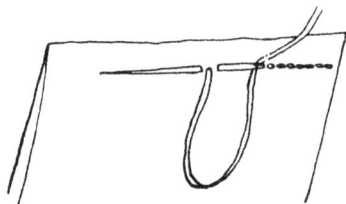

Back Stitch

The back stitch is a hand-made stitch which on the right side looks like machine stitching. It should be about the size of machine stitching and as even and straight. Work from right to left on the right side of the fabric. Start by making a small stitch on the wrong side at the right hand end of the work. Make a stitch on top of this one but on the right side, sticking the needle down through the hole at the beginning of the first stitch, but this time bring it out the length of the stitch ahead of the end of the first stitch (see Fig. 10). Continue putting the needle back to last stitch each time so that there is no space between stitches.

This stitch is used where strength is needed in a hand-made seam and where it is not easy to use a sewing machine.

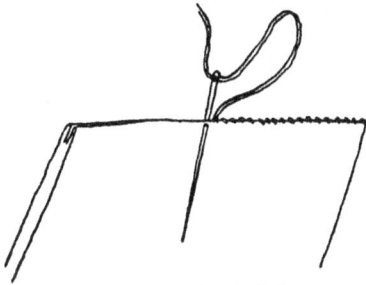

Fig. 11.—Overhand stitch.

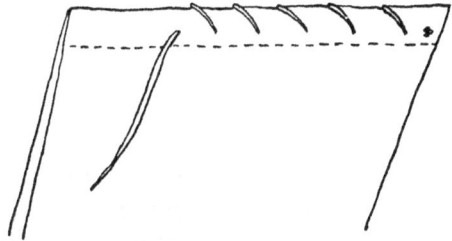

Fig. 12.—Overcasting stitch.

Overhand Stitch

The overhand stitch is a short stitch used to hold two folded edges together. On the one side the stitches are at right angles to the edges; on the other side they slant across the edges. Overhand stitches should show very little from either right or wrong side. They should be the same length, slant the same way and be the same distance apart. The edges to be joined should be basted together, with folded edges even. Hold the work between the thumb and first finger of the left hand, with folded edges up. Always work from right to left. Fasten thread with two or three stitches on top of each other. Holding needle at right angles to the edge, insert it in the fabric, picking up only a thread or two of both folded edges (Fig. 11), and draw it through. Make each stitch in the same way. The thread should be loose enough that the edge does not pucker, but tight enough that the stitches will sink into the cloth.

This stitch is used to join selvages or folded edges together, such as ends of hems in towels, or to join lace to a hem.

Overcasting Stitch

The overcasting stitch is a slanting stitch made over a raw edge to keep it from raveling. The stitch looks the same on both sides except the stitches slant in opposite directions. The work may be done from left to right, but it can be done more quickly and easily by working from right to left. Hold the work between the left forefinger and thumb.

To start, fasten the thread with a small hidden knot. Throwing needle and thread over edge of fabric, stick the needle through the fabric, from the underside, pointing needle toward the left shoulder, and bring it through to the upper side. This makes a slanting stitch over the edge of the fabric. The loop of thread over the edge should be drawn tightly, but not tight enough to pucker the edge. The stitches should be about the same length and distance apart as those shown in Fig. 12. Each stitch may be made one at a time or several stitches may be taken on the needle at one time. In either case, keep thread loose enough that edge will not curl.

This stitch is used to keep raw edges from raveling, as on raw edge of a plain seam.

Blanket Stitch

The blanket stitch may be made over a hemmed edge or a raw edge of wool or firm fabric that will not ravel easily. The stitches should be even in length, the same distance apart, and at right angles to the edge. Use cotton embroidery thread. Work from left to right, with the material held along the

Fig. 13.—Blanket stitch.

first finger of the left hand and with the edge to be blanket stitched turned toward you. Fasten thread with small knot or back stitches made over the edge. Bring the needle out on the edge to be finished.

Holding thread under thumb of left hand, place point of needle down in fabric the width of a narrow hem, or about ¼ inch from a raw edge. Bring needle out from under side of fabric and over the thread held under the thumb. The needle passes through a loop of thread each time it is drawn from the fabric. Make each stitch the same way, sticking the needle down in the fabric to the right of stitch just made. The stitches are usually a little less than ¼ inch apart. Fasten thread on wrong side with a few short stitches.

The blanket stitch is used to hold narrow hems in place, to finish raw edges, and as trimming.

The hemming stitch is a small stitch made on the first turn of a twice folded edge. Hold the turned edge wrong side up across the first finger of the left hand, with the second turn or outside edge toward the palm of the hand. Start with a small knot in the thread and hide it under the folded edge.

1. *Slant Hemming.* — Make a short slanting stitch by first sticking needle in the fabric close to the edge of hem and a little to the left of where the thread is fastened. Catch a few threads of the fabric. Slant needle into edge of hem and pick up a few threads of the fold (Fig. 14). Draw the needle through. Make each stitch in same way. The needle is always slanted toward the left shoulder. The stitches should be small (about ⅛ inch), the same distance apart, and should show little on either right or wrong side of work. To fasten thread when finished, take two or three stitches on top of each other in folded edge.

This stitch is used to hold hems, facings, and bindings in place.

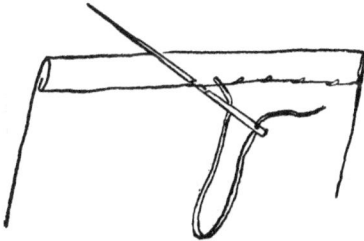

Fig. 14.—Slant hemming.

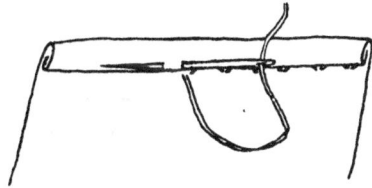

Fig. 15.—Slip stitch hemming.

2. *Slip-stitch Hemming.* — Bring the needle out of the first fold and take a small stitch in fabric in line with the place where thread is fastened, catching only a thread or two of the fabric. Stick the needle again in folded edge to the left of the stitch first made and slip it forward within the fold from ¼ to ½ inch (Fig. 15). This stitch should be hidden in the edge of the hem on the wrong side. On the right side the stitches are small, even in size and spacing, and show little.

The slip-stitch is used to hold hems or facings or any edge in place, where a neat finish is desired on both wrong and right sides.

Edge Finishes

Plain Seam

To make a plain seam, place the two right sides of the fabric together, raw edges even. Baste ¼ to ⅜ inch from raw edges. Stitch by hand or machine along line of basting. Remove basting and press the seam flat with the two raw edges together. If the wrong side of the seam may show from the right side, overcast (page 24) the raw edges to keep them from raveling. This seam is used to join two edges when a flat seam is needed.

Plain Hem

Trim raw edges evenly. Crease edge about ¼ inch to wrong side. Make a cardboard gage (see page 7) the width you wish the hem to be. Measure, turn, crease, and baste hem in place carefully. Hand hem narrow hems in place with the slant hemming stitch (page 26).

Napery or Damask Hem

Fold a narrow plain hem. Baste hem in place. Then fold hem back against right side of fabric, creasing the fabric even with first fold of hem (Fig. 16). Overhand (page 23) the folded edges together. Open hem out and press it flat. The napery hem is used on towels and table linens.

Fig. 16.—Damask or napery hem.

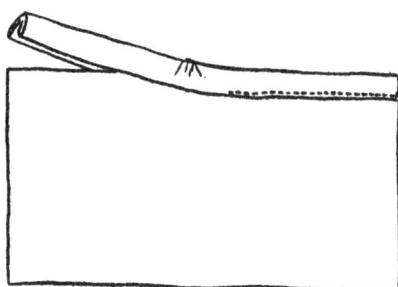

Fig. 17.—Straight or flat binding.

Bias Binding

Use double fold ready-made bias, or fold flat bias through the center so that one-half of the binding is a thread wider than the other. With wider side of binding to wrong side of fabric, slip binding over edge to be bound (Fig. 17). Baste and stitch from right side along edge of binding.

To Join Bias Strips.— Cut ends of bias strips on a thread of the fabric. Place the two pieces together so that they form a right angle (Fig. 18a). Baste and stitch a plain seam. Press seam open and cut off corners even with edge of bias (Fig. 18b). If ends of binding are to meet on the edge of an article, measure length of bias strip needed. Join the two ends together, before basting binding to edge of an article.

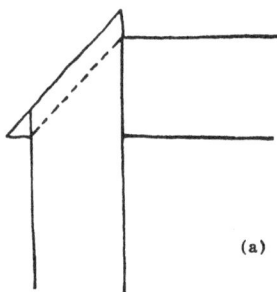

(a)

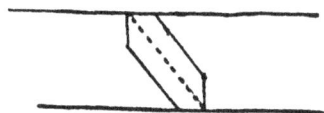

(b)

Fig. 18.—Method of joining bias strips.

26

4-H Homemaking Projects for Girls

Four-H homemaking projects include, in addition to those in clothing listed below, projects in foods and nutrition; home furnishings, and home management. Special projects and discussion outlines for older girls 15 to 20 years of age, inclusive, are Series I and II, Personality Development; When 4-H Club Members Entertain; and Looking Your Best.

CLOTHING PROJECTS

For Girls 11 to 14 Years, Inclusive

11 and 12 years of age:

> The A, B, C's of Sewing for the 4-H Club Girl.
> Arrange sewing basket.
> Make at least three useful articles.
> Complete circular by filling in blanks.

> The 4-H Club Girl Learns to Sew.
> Arrange sewing basket.
> Make at least three useful articles or toys.
> Complete circular by filling in blanks.

12 through 14 years of age:

> Dresses for Home and Play
> Make at least one dress.
> Mend and care for her home and play dresses.
> Complete circular by filling in blanks.

> Undergarments for the 4-H Club Girl
> Make at least two undergarments.
> Mend and care for her undergarments.
> Complete circular by filling in blanks.

> The 4-H Club Girl's Dresses for School, Business, Sports, Street.
> Make at least one dress.
> Mend and care for her school and sports dresses.
> Complete circular by filling in blanks.

Projects for older girls on page 28

The 4-H Club Girls' Dresses for School, Business, Sports, and Street
Make at least one dress.
Mend and care for her school and sports dresses.
Complete circular by filling in blanks.

The 4-H Club Girl's Dress-up Dresses.
Make at least one dress.
Mend and care for her dress-up dresses.
Complete circular by filing in blanks.

The Older 4-H Club Girls' Complete Costume.
Plan and make a complete costume for an occasion selected by the girl.
Make the dress and undergarments. Select foundation, hose, shoes, and
other accessories needed to complete the costume.
Complete circular by filling in blanks.

To Wash Soiled Articles

Wash carefully in two suds, using lukewarm water and a mild white soap; rinse until the last rinse water is clear. Dry until only damp enough to iron. Carefully test temperature of iron. Press article until dry and free from wrinkles. For pincushions and bean bags, be sure the fabric is clean and well pressed before stuffing.

4-H Clothing Projects

The Well Dressed 4-H Club Girl's

Dress-up Dresses

_____
Name of Member

_____
Age

_____
Address of Member

_____
Name of Club

_____
Advisor's Name

Cooperative Extension Work in Agriculture and Home Economics, State of Ohio
The Ohio State University and the United States Department of Agriculture Cooperating
Agl. Extension Service: Department 4-H Club Work—W. H. Palmer, State Club Leader

EXTENSION SERVICE OF THE COLLEGE OF AGRICULTURE
THE OHIO STATE UNIVERSITY
COLUMBUS

Dear 4-H Club Member:

As you attend your local 4-H Club meetings isn't it thrilling to know that in far-off Hawaii or Alaska, and also in every state in the United States, girls just like you are also attending 4-H Club meetings! You have heard it said "A chain is as strong as its weakest link." You are a link in the "chain" of 4-H Clubs in your county. Your club will be only as strong as you, one of the links, make it. Have you asked yourself this question: "How can I make my 4-H Club a real 4-H Club?"

4-H Club work all over this country of ours is unique in that every member of the 4-H Club group has a home making project for which she is responsible.

You are a member of a family group. Have you ever thought how your project may help some member of your family, or help you to be a better member of your family than you are now?

How we all like to dress up in dress-up dresses now and then and go to something special and different than everyday happenings!

May you enjoy your membership in your 4-H Club and the making of a dress-up dress!

Sincerely yours,

Hulda Horst

Assistant State 4-H Club Leader

The Pledge

I pledge my head to clearer thinking, my heart to greater loyalty, my hands to larger service, my health to better living, for my club, my community, and my country.

△

National 4-H Club Girl's Song

My home must have a high tree
Above its open gate.
My home must have a garden
Where little dreamings wait,
My home must have a wide view
Of field and meadow fair
Of distant hill, of open sky
With sunlight everywhere.

—Buchanan-Parish

△

What Each 4-H Club Does

Each club group

1. Has an adult advisor who guides the group.
2. Has a definite organization with constitution and officers.
3. Plans a local club program based on needs of the group, which program includes
    a. Regular meetings with time for business, project work, and recreation.
    b. The activities planned by the county, such as camps, tours, trips, county exhibits.
    c. A health program.
    d. A community service program.
    e. The local achievement meeting.
    f. State activities such as Ohio Club Congress and Junior Fair.
4. Makes an exhibit, locally.

I. As a Member of a Local 4-H Club Group:

1. Attends local club meetings and other activities such as trips, tours, county meetings, local and county exhibits, and achievement day.

2. Helps to plan the local 4-H club program and takes part in carrying it out; serves as an officer or on committees.

3. Takes part in a group health program.

4. Takes part in a group community service program.

5. Plans, carries on, and completes at least one 4-H homemaking project and keeps her record during the time when the club group is carrying on the project.

II. Each 4-H Club Girl in Her Project:

1. Reads this circular and fills in some of the questions on pages 20 to 30 at or before each 4-H club meeting.

2. Plans and makes at least one dress for dress-up wear. (She may make more if she wishes.) See pages 10 and 16.

3. Purchases or helps with the purchase of patterns, fabrics, and trimmings (see pages 10 to 14).

4. Provides own sewing supplies and equipment (see pages 3 and 4 of Garment Construction).

5. Uses the sewing machine. (see page 22).

6. Cares for her dress-up dress; stores, removes spots and stains, and makes necessary repairs (see pages 17 to 19).

7. Practices good posture and good grooming at all times (see pages 6 to 10).

8. Wears her dress and with the help of her club checks it using the check sheet (see page 27).

9. Completes and checks records in back of this circular (pages 20 to 30).

10. Wears her dress-up dress at the time of the local judging and brings the completed 4-H circular.

The Well Dressed 4-H Club Girl's Dress-up Dresses

By Edna M. Callahan and Edith Berry

Extension Specialists in Clothing, the Ohio State University

A r no time is a girl more interested in her appearance than when she dresses up for a social event. But the dress she dons is not the only thing that counts at such a time. Every 4-H club girl who wants to make a pleasing appearance will strive to have good health so that she feels well; she will groom herself carefully and wear becoming clothes so that she looks well; she will select clothes that are suitable for the different functions she attends so that she may be comfortable and have a good time; and she will cultivate a pleasing personality so that folks will like her.

Not everyone needs the same number or kind of dress-up dresses. Some occasions requiring such dresses are church, calling, special club, school, or community meetings, informal teas, neighborhood parties or other informal daytime parties,. dinners, banquets, and evening parties. On such occasions as these a girl appreciates the importance of contributing her part socially so she tries to look her best. For this reason, every 4-H club girl needs to have a wearable dress in her wardrobe which will be suitable for most of the dress-up occasions which she will be attending. Most girls do not need a dressier dress than the afternoon type which is suitable for church, and for informal afternoon and evening functions. A few girls may find they have use for simple informal party dresses appropriate for more dressy evening parties.

The dress-up dress need not be elaborate. It may get its dressed-up appearance from either the design or the fabric used, or from both. This type of dress may be made of dainty cotton fabric or of rayon or silk. It should be becoming, well made, graceful in line, and stylish. Although dressier than the dress intended for school, business, sports, or street wear, the dressy dress need not be expensive. It should, however, show thoughtful planning and careful workmanship.

Every 4-H club girl who is interested in this project will want to read this circular carefully and discuss the suggestions therein at home and in club meetings. She will want to make a dress-up dress for herself; check her posture and follow good grooming practices on all occasions; and also take proper care of her dress-up dresses.

The 4-H Club Girl's Dresses for Dress-up Occasions

A GIRL's APPEARANCE in a dressy dress is especially dependent upon the way she stands, sits, and walks, and on how well groomed she is.

A Well Poised, Graceful Body.—A good, erect posture helps to give poise and self-confidence which are essential to social success. The girl whose posture passes as fair in a loosely fitted sports frock may be surprised when she sees herself in a well fitted dress-up dress. For her flat chest, prominent abdomen, hollow back, and general unsightly slouch makes it impossible for her to look well in the most beautiful and most becoming dress-up dress. Good posture is a necessary part of good looks. A girl who carries herself well stands so that a plumb line dropped from the side of the head will pass through the middle of her ear, shoulder, hip, knee, and outer ankle bone (see Fig. 1). She can stand, walk, sit, and even climb

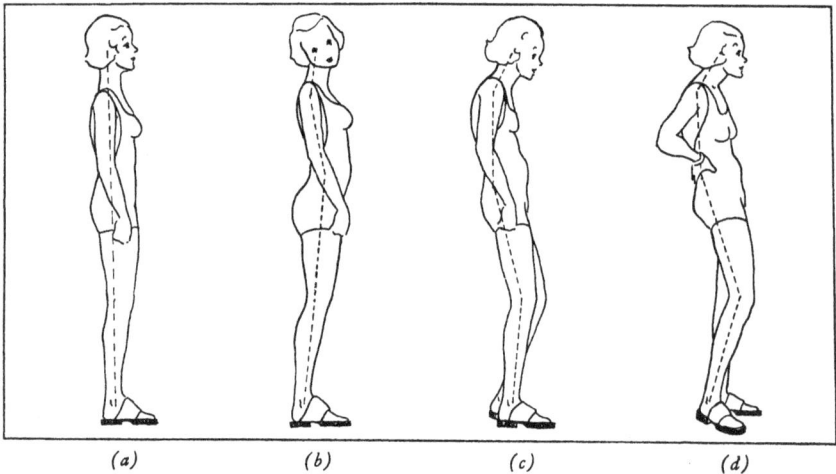

(a)　　　　*(b)*　　　　*(c)*　　　　*(d)*

Fig. 1.—*(a)* Good posture, well poised body; *(b)* exaggerated back hollow, relaxed abdomen; *(c)* poor posture, flat chest, prominent abdomen;*(d)* unsightly slouch, head forward, chest flat, protruding abdomen.

stairs with a book balanced on top of her head without first changing the way her body is lined up. Such a posture as this can give grace, style, and smartness to a very simple dress.

A Clean Body.—Society is extremely severe in its criticism of body odor or soiled clothing, especially for dress-up occasions. Fortunately, in this modern day, it is possible for every girl to be neat and fresh in appearance if she is willing to give a reasonable amount of time and thought to her personal grooming and the care of her clothes.

Every girl can add to her attractiveness by keeping herself clean. So important is this matter of cleanliness that it is practically impossible for a girl to be charming and dainty unless her body is clean. Therefore, frequent bathing is necessary to a pleasing appearance. In addition to the usual bathing routine, a sponge or tub bath taken just before dressing for a dress-up occasion usually adds to a person's comfort and good time. Dusting powder, used after the bath, helps to retain a clean fresh feeling for a short time, but if one perspires easily, a deodorant such as zinc stearate, baking soda dissolved in water, or a commercial preparation may be used to prevent objectionable body odors. Astringents to check perspiration may be purchased, and if used according to directions they will protect clothing from stains and odors of perspiration as well as assure the user a fresh feeling and appearance. However, if they irritate the skin they should not be used. The effect of these non-perspirants for the average person usually lasts for two or three days.

An Attractive Face.—Today the fashion in faces is a natural rather than an artificial effect. Glowing health is the first and most important aid to this natural beauty. The healthy, active 4-H club girl who has a lovely complexion with clear, firm skin, pink cheeks, and red lips is fortunate and has a gift that should be carefully guarded. Poor health practices such as faulty diet and improper elimination are quickly reflected in the face, causing the skin to become coarse and rough and blemishes to appear from time to time. Such troubles are ordinarily corrected through proper diet, drinking plenty of water, out-of-door exercise, and plenty of sleep.

Another important beauty rule is keeping the face clean, for keeping the skin clean both protects a lovely complexion and improves a poor one. Frequent and regular washings with a pure mild soap and warm water followed by several clear, cold rinses is the ideal treatment and is easily done. The face should always be cleaned each night before going to bed and always before applying make-up.

Since cosmetics are being used so extensively today it might be well to consider their correct use. Every girl needs to decide for herself whether or not she will use make-up. If she decides to use it then she will need to decide on what kind to use and how to apply it. It seems too bad for the girl with a lovely complexion to spoil it with obvious make-up. It does not follow that all pale girls improve their appearance by the use of make-up. For example, a girl with lovely eyes, pale cheeks and lips might detract from the beauty of her eyes by overshadowing them with vivid cheeks and lips. If the cheeks and lips are pale, giving a tired, unhealthy appearance, a touch of rouge and lipstick may be used to advantage. All make-up used should contribute to a natural, healthy appearance. This means that rouge and powder will need to match or blend with the natural coloring, and be applied carefully so that a girl will look like herself, only nicer, and her family and friends will be proud of her loveliness. Since artificial light subdues and sometimes changes colors, a little more make-up may be used for evening parties. When buying make-up, it is well to notice what effect artificial light has upon it.

Make-up is a means whereby the apparent shape of the face, if needed, may be improved. If the face is broad, rouge placed fairly close to the nose and no wider than the width of three fingers held in an upright position under the eye makes it appear narrower.

If the face is narrow, the rouge confined to a small area around the cheek bones, but blended out over the cheeks toward the ears, gives an effect of greater width.

If the face is long and oval, the rouge should be applied far out on the cheek bones, and blended outward toward the ears, keeping it well away from the nose.

Rouge should be confined to the upper part of the face, otherwise it may accent the jaw line, deepen hollows in the cheeks, and give a drawn expression.

The apparent shape of the mouth may be improved, too, if needed, by the way the lip rouge is applied. When using lipstick the lips should be dry. The color is then applied to the upper lip and transferred to the lower one by pressing the lips together. Lip rouge should be smoothed and blended with the tip of the finger to be sure the lips are evenly covered and that there are no hard lines around the outer edges of the mouth. As a final step, cleaning tissue pressed to the lips will remove the surplus lipstick and prevent the lips from looking caked or oily.

If the lips are wide and full the rouge should not be spread to the outer edges. For full lips, color should be applied heavier on the upper lip than on the lower one. Thin and narrow lips appear wider when the deepest color is carried to their outer edges.

Bright, Clear, Attractive Eyes.—Good health, happiness, and enough rest help to keep the eyes clear and bright. The well-groomed girl gives some thought to her eyebrows, for they play an important part in the expression of her face. For a pleasant expression, brows should not meet over the nose. If they have a tendency to meet, a small space may be plucked to make a distinct separation between them. Naturally heavy brows should be left heavy, but they will look better if kept in line by plucking the straggling hairs on each side. Care should be taken not to pluck too many as this will give an artificial look. Always before plucking hair from the skin the area around the hair, the fingers, and the tweezers should be sterilized with rubbing alcohol as there is danger of infection. If the brows are so light that they do not show at all, an eyebrow pencil of the same color as the hair may be used to accent the brow line. The pencil should be used on the hair and not on the skin, and the effect must be natural if it is to be in good taste.

Attractive Hands and Nails.—Sometimes hands speak more eloquently than words to express a girl's taste. Her hands may not be shapely, but if they are clean, smooth, and free from stains, the nails clean and well shaped, they express refinement. Hand lotion kept in a convenient place is easily applied when needed. Lemon juice or peroxide may be used to remove stains from the hands and stains from under the nails. Well manicured nails are shaped to conform with the shape of the fingertips and kept free from ragged cuticle. It is a good practice to take an extra minute, when drying the hands, to push back the cuticle from each nail with the towel.

The only tools needed to care for the hands and nails are: a nail brush, a nail file, and an orange stick. Nail polish is often used on the nails for dress-up wear, but on most other occasions, it is not necessary. Natural colored polish is usually in much better taste than the brilliant tones.

A Girl's Crowning Glory.—Well-groomed hair is just as essential as well-groomed hands, and both are highly important on dress-up occasions. Well-groomed hair is scrupulously clean and glossy. Hair in normal condition should be brushed thoroughly once a day to help keep it clean and make it glossy. The best style of hair dress for a girl is sometimes determined by the occasion. For instance, if she is going to church or to a community party, she may dress her hair much as she would for school or street wear (see Fig. 2). If attending a party, she may prefer

8

a hairdress with soft waves to give a dressier effect. It is better to choose a simple arrangement rather than an elaborate one which may require too much attention. If the hair is worn short, regular visits to a barber or hairdresser are necessary to keep the hairline neat and well trimmed.

To make sure that her hair is doing the most for her appearance, a girl should try various arrangements, such as parting her hair in different places, placing the bulk of the hair high, medium, or low, bringing it over the face, and combing it back, exposing the hair line, until a style is found which is becoming to her size, features, and personality.

Since the oval face is considered ideal, girls with faces which are too round or too slender should try particularly hard to find a style of hairdress which will make their faces appear more oval. For example, the girl with a high forehead usually finds that dipping the hair over each eye shortens the forehead. The square face looks best with a fluffy hair style. Loose waves also soften the features. The small face appears fuller when the hair is parted in the middle. Only girls with perfect features wear a severely plain hairdress becomingly.

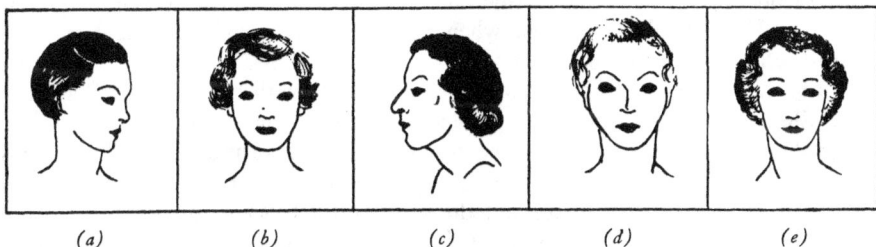

(a)   (b)   (c)   (d)   (e)

Fig. 2.—Becoming hair arrangements for: (a) straight hair; (b) curly hair; (c) large nose; (d) wide face; (e) long thin face.

Size and personality should also be considered. A large girl will do well to wear her hair smooth and close to her head, while the girl who is small in size for her age, may wear the fluffy type of hairdress.

The dainty, lively girl may wear a dressier hairdress than the dignified girl, who wears best the smooth, dignified styles. The athletic girl usually finds a simple, sports-type of hairdress most becoming for all occasions.

A Pleasant Smile.—Nothing can mar a pleasant smile more completely than unsightly teeth. Clean, attractive teeth help add to a girl's poise and self-assurance. This means that aside from the two or three brushings a girl gives her teeth daily, she should brush them again when grooming herself for dress-up occasions. She may wish to follow this extra brushing with a good mouth wash. This can be made at home of a little salt or soda dissolved in water.

Every 4-H club girl should visit her dentist to check up on whether or not she is giving her teeth the right kind of care and to keep her teeth in good repair.

Clothes Play their Part.—If a girl is to have a dainty, attractive appearance on dress-up occasions, her hose and all her undergarments must be clean. If she has a limited supply of these garments, she will have to plan carefully in order to have them clean for each wearing. This may mean that some washing will need to be done each day.

It is best to wash better undergarments and hose by hand, using a mild, white soap and lukewarm water, and to rinse them in several clear, cold waters.

If the foundation garment is worn for dress-up occasions, it may be worn several times before washing. It should be washed whenever it is soiled, and should be washed the same as undergarments, being sure that the water used is cool or less than lukewarm. Foundation garments should be dried away from heat and sun, and the elastic parts should never be pressed with an iron.

No matter how lovely a costume is, a girl never feels or looks dressed up if her dress is soiled or wrinkled. Dress-up dresses may be worn several times without cleaning or washing if they are carefully pressed before they are worn and protected between wearings. Directions for washing, ironing, pressing, and covering dresses are given in this circular, page 17. Every girl wants to look and feel as if "she had just stepped out of a bandbox," and to do this, she must pay strict attention to details. Good grooming includes so many things. Runners in hose, loose buttons, ripped stitches, and frayed edges will detract from an otherwise well-groomed appearance. Therefore, ripped seams should be restitched, frayed edges mended, and worn-out elastic shoulder straps and hand stitches replaced promptly. Hose should be darned when they wear thin, and snags and runners mended when they begin to appear.

The way a girl wears her clothes has much to do with her "bandbox" appearance. She should keep her lingerie straps in place by means of holders attached to the shoulder seams of her dresses. She should have adjustable shoulder straps on her slips to keep them from hanging below her dresses. Her stockings must be free from wrinkles at the ankles and the seams must be kept straight. Her shoe-strings should be tied securely so they will not become loose or untied. When putting on her dress she should adjust it till it sits properly on her shoulders. Her belt should be straight and in place. If the end of the belt is long, it should be fastened to the belt with a snap fastener. Any bows should be neatly tied. In fact, no matter how trivial the details may seem, they must receive attention, for otherwise a well-groomed appearance is impossible.

△

The 4-H Club Girl Plans Her Dressy Dress

*A*NY GIRL, when correctly dressed, feels more at ease and has a better time than when she is inappropriately dressed for the occasion. This is why both the planning and the wearing of the dress-up dress is important. In general, a dressy dress differs from a school or street dress in that the material is more dressy, the design less tailored, the construction finer, and the trimming (if used) more elegant.

Dress Design.—If the 4-H club girl intends to wear her dress-up dress for church, community gatherings, and similar occasions, the design need not be much different from that of her school, sports, or street dresses. However if she goes to several informal parties, she may need to make a dressier dress for party wear (see Fig. 3).

Dressy dresses may or may not follow the outline of the figure. For instance, flared skirts, cape collars, and wide sleeves, which are used on dressy dresses, do not cling to the figure as do plaited skirts, fitted sleeves, and narrow roll collars, which are more often used on the tailored dress. The lines within a dressy dress are usually soft and graceful rather than straight and tailored. The length of the dress may or may not be longer than the tailored dress. This depends upon the fashion, the style of the dress, the size and age of the girl, as well as the occasions for which the dress is planned. The party dress is usually a little longer than one worn on other dress-up occasions.

Regardless of the type of dress worn, the face should always be the center of interest. A becoming neckline, an interesting collar, vest, or yoke, or a contrasting color used at the neckline helps to direct attention toward the face rather than to some part of the costume.

(a)   (b)   (c)

Fig. 3.—(a) dress-up dress for church and afternoon wear; (b) dress-up dress for party wear; (c) party dress for dressy evening parties.

The girl with an average figure may choose any good design she wishes, provided it is suitable for the use she intends it, and will look well with the other garments and accessories she has to wear with it. This is not possible for the short, stout girl, who is too wide for her height, for she must look for slenderizing lines in the dress pattern. She should look for long unbroken lines from shoulder to lower edge of skirt, such as: narrow panels, narrow vests, long or pointed narrow collars, narrow necklines, longer skirts with narrow groups of plaits, close fitting sleeves, belts which match the dress, and fitted beltless dresses.

The tall, slender girl, who is too tall for her width, on the other hand, should look for designs which will make her look shorter such as: circular flounces, wide skirt hems, wide panels, draped collars and sleeves, broad necklines and collars, full blouses, yokes, tunics, boleros, crosswise tucks, capes, soft wide belts, or those of contrasting material, full sleeves, wide cuffs and cuffs of contrasting material.

Some girls, although very tall and slender, have broad hips and they have still another problem. They will want to look for designs which broaden the upper part of the figure and slenderize the hips. Other girls are larger above than below the waist. They should choose designs with up-and-down lines through the shoulders and crosswise lines over the hips.

Necklines, when properly selected, can do a great deal to make the face which is not a perfect oval assume more perfect proportions. The broad face appears less broad when V-shaped and narrow U-shaped necklines are worn, while the square and broad U-shaped necklines make the long, slender face appear more round (see Fig. 4).

The personality of the wearer should also play a part in the selection of a pattern. For instance, dainty, feminine girls usually look well in frilly designs, while boyish, athletic girls look awkward in long, ruffled, fussy dresses. Plain, simple, tailored dresses are best suited to the athletic type. Likewise, the dignified or dramatic type of girl should choose a plain design rather than a fussy one.

Conservative designs are the most economical choices for dressy dresses. Since this type of dress is not worn, it should last two or more seasons. Fashion fads are extravagant, since they last no more than one season.

| (a) | (b) | (c) |

Fig. 4.—(a) high round necklines are becoming to the long slender face; (b) the oval face may wear most any shaped neckline; (c) the V-shaped neckline is becoming to the broad face.

The care of a dress should also be considered when selecting the design. It may be important to select a design which will not be difficult to wash and which can be ironed and pressed successfully. For instance, ribbon belts do not wash well and many ruffles are difficult to iron.

Further help with selecting and using a pattern may be found in "Garment Construction," page 5.

Color for the Dress-up Dress.—Almost any light or dark color which is dull or medium in brightness is suitable for a dressy dress. It is usually best to avoid bright, showy colors. Cool colors, such as blue and green, look cooler for summer wear; and violet, red, and orange look warmer for winter wear. However, the light values of these warm colors are suitable for summer dresses, and the dark values of the cool colors are excellent for winter wear. For instance, pink, which is a tint of red, is a suitable summer color, and dark green or blue may be worn in winter or summer.

Without doubt, the most important consideration when selecting color for a dress is its becomingness to the individual girl. In order to decide which colors are most becoming, a girl should hold various colors next to her face and observe their effect in a well lighted mirror. She should also notice what each color does to the rest of her body. It may make her appear larger or smaller, and her hair more or less colorful. A small or average size girl may wear almost any color which is becoming to her coloring and personality, but the large girl should avoid large masses of intense color; that is especially true of the warm colors.

Subdued colors, including light, delicate tones, deep, rich colors, and dark, grayed ones, are easier to wear than bright, intense colors. Many times a touch of intense color is becoming, while an entire dress of the same color would be unbecoming. Also girls tire of conspicuous colors more quickly than they do of soft, subdued colors.

A girl has an excellent opportunity to work out pleasing color harmonies when planning a dressy dress. She should take into account the color of the other garments and accessories which are to be worn with the dress. The dress may match, harmonize, or form a contrast with the hat, gloves, coat, hose, and shoes. Also, if a printed fabric is desired for the dress, a print with colors which look pretty together should be selected. Such combinations as light values of brown (orange), yellow-green (which is both yellow and green), and blue on a white background should make a pleasing combination.

Fabrics for the Dress-up Dress.—The material from which a dressy dress is made has much to do with its becomingness. Shiny fabrics reflect light and thereby increase the apparent size of the wearer. For this reason only slender, well proportioned girls can wear shiny surfaced fabrics, such as satin and metal cloth, becomingly. Dull fabrics, on the other hand, are becoming to most girls, for they have a tendency to decrease the apparent size of the wearer and make her appear more slender. Most cottons, silk crepes, and linens are dull surfaced fabrics.

Stiff fabrics conceal the outline of the figure but they stand away from the figure, thereby increasing its apparent size; for this reason stiff fabrics such as taffeta and organdie should be avoided by the large girl. Such fabrics need to be handled carefully or they will emphasize any harsh or angular lines of the figure as well as make it look larger. Soft fabrics are much more becoming to the large figure. Some soft fabrics are crepes, sheers, cotton lace, voiles, and soft muslins.

If the fabric has design, the pattern and color of the design are also important to becomingness. Large designs of bright colors and striking color contrasts, and especially large oval or round motifs, make the wearer appear larger, and should be avoided by the short, too-wide figure. Instead, she should wear soft fabrics, all-over designs, pin stripes, or plain colors.

The too-thin girl has more freedom in her choice of both texture and design. She would do well to avoid pin stripes, however, and to make sure the design she chooses is in scale with her size and proportions.

Every girl, when selecting the fabric for a dress-up dress, should think of the amount of care it will require. One simple test is to pull a sample of the fabric between the thumbs and forefingers. If the threads slip easily, then a dress made of the fabric will probably pull out at seams and places of strain, where repairs are difficult to make. Fabrics which are color fast and easy to wash and iron are a pleasure to own. This is true of many of the cottons which, in general, are easier to care for than silks and rayons. A girl should notice when selecting her fabric whether or not there is anything which can be pulled off easily, such as paste dots imitating dotted swiss, or designs pasted on to voile, for these may fall off in washing and are often discolored by pressing.

Printed fabrics may be more practical than plain colors because they show soil and spots less readily, yet plain colors of medium value are more wearable throughout the year.

Some fabrics which should be satisfactory for dress-up dresses are dimity, dotted swiss, lawn, voile, sheer cotton prints, batiste, French gingham, cotton lace, organdie, and washable silks and rayons. Taffeta, crepes, and novelty silks and rayons are also suitable for dress-up wear, but these fabrics usually require dry cleaning.

Every girl should be able to recognize dotted swiss and organdie when she sees them. True dotted swiss has embroidered dots, and they usually wear better than the dots which are pressed onto the fabric. Dimity may be recognized by the small cordlike threads running lengthwise of the fabric. These threads or stripes are the same color as the background color of the fabric. Lawn, batiste, voile, and sheer prints are smooth, plain weave, sheer fabrics. Lawn is stiff, but not as stiff as organdie; batiste is soft; and voile is made of hard twisted threads which give it a hard feel. Tissue gingham is sheer, also, but usually has stripes or checks woven in the fabric. Silk and rayon can often be distinguished by the feel and appearance. Silk has a gloss, and unless it is heavily weighted, is soft and light in weight. Rayon has either a brilliant or dull metallic luster, and usually feels wiry, non-elastic, slippery, cool and smooth.

△

The 4-H Club Girl Makes Her Dress-up Dress

*A*s was stated before in this circular, the construction of a dress-up dress is important, since a well made dress helps the wearer to feel well dressed. Some suitable kinds of dress finishes are suggested here. For methods of making these finishes, the 4-H club member should refer to the bulletin, "Garment Construction."

Preparation of the Fabric.—Cotton and washable rayon fabrics which are not pre-shrunk should be shrunk before cutting out the dress. The directions in Garment Construction under "Preparing Material and Laying on the Pattern," page 10, and "Shrinking the Material," page 11, should be read.

Cutting, Basting and Fitting.—The directions in Garment Construction under "Cutting and Marking," page 13; "Assembling the Parts of the Garment," "Fitting the Garment," page 14; and "The Finishing Touches," page 16, should be read carefully before the garment is cut out.

Seams.—French seams are probably the most satisfactory for the straight seams in sheer fabrics which are apt to fray badly. French seams in sheer fabrics do not need to be wider than ⅛ to 3⁄16 inch, and are much neater when narrow. Directions for making French seams are given in Garment Construction, page 29. Lap seams are used for joining yokes, panels, gores, etc.; directions for making are given in Garment Construction, page 28. Imitation French seams may be used for armseye seams in sheer fabrics; see page 28, Garment Construction.

Silk and rayon fabrics are seldom transparent so may be made with plain seams, page 26, Garment Construction. Plain seams should measure $\frac{3}{8}$ to $\frac{1}{2}$ inch in width unless the material frays badly or is loosely woven then they may be wider. The edges of the plain seams should be finished as recommended in Garment Construction, page 26.

Hems.—Hems in a dressy dress should always be put in by hand. They may be $2\frac{1}{2}$ to 3 inches in width unless the skirt is very full, and circular, then a $\frac{1}{8}$-inch creased or rolled hem looks better and is easier to turn. Directions under "Hems and Their Finishes" in Garment Construction, page 30, should be read and also "Vertical or Straight Hemming," top of page 21.

Waistline Finishes.—Some fitted dresses, including those which are fitted by groups of tucks at the waistline, do not need a belt. Other dresses need a belt to add a note of interest to the dress, or, for the tall figure, to break the length of the dress.

Belts made of the same material as the dress are inconspicuous and becoming to the stout figure. Belts of contrasting material, such as plain brown linen on a brown and white print dress, tend to make the figure look broader and shorter, and are worn best by the tall, slender girl. Soft sashes with tied ends are suitable for dressy dresses and some of the belts made of crocheted yarns or grosgrain ribbon are very appropriate.

All belts should be attached to the dress in some manner. For this purpose straps made of the dress fabric or thread loops may be attached at each side seam, or swing tacks may be used. Directions for making these fasteners are given in Garment Construction, page 44.

Neck Finishes.—Collars, of either the same fabric as the dress or contrasting material, make attractive neck finishes. Usually a collar is more becoming than a plain neckline because the collar frames the face and helps to make it the center of interest. Non-convertible collars are the type usually used on dressy dresses. Directions for applying collars are given in Garment Construction, pages 43 and 44.

A dress of dressy design which is made of dainty fabric may be finished at the neckline with lace edging or a lacy collar.

A double bias binding or French bias is a suitable neckline finish for a collarless dress. The binding is usually made of the same fabric as the dress, although for a printed dress the binding may be of a plain material which matches the background color of the print. Directions for making and applying bias bindings are given in Garment Construction, page 32.

Armseye Finishes.—Set-in sleeves, shoulder caps, and cape collars, extending over the upper part of the arm, are suitable for a dressy dress. Set-in sleeves may be short or long, depending upon the season for which the dress is intended, the design of the dress, and the size of the girl. A shoulder cap, which is a shaped piece, is set on over the outer edge of the shoulder of the dress. Directions for attaching the caps are usually included with the pattern. Large cape collars are becoming to the tall, slender girl because they tend to broaden and shorten the figure. The method to use in setting in sleeves is given in Garment Construction, foot of page 17. Directions for applying other sleeve finishes may be found with the pattern.

Skirt Fullness.—Plaits and circular flares are devices used to give fullness to an otherwise straight skirt. Some skirts are cut on the bias or are gored to give fullness. Methods of adding plaits and flares to skirts are given in Garment Construction, page 42.

Plackets.—The fitted dress calls for a placket opening at the waistline and often at the neck to enable the wearer to put on and take off the dress easily. The short neck opening may be faced, bound like a buttonhole, or bound with a bias binding or French bias. The long placket may extend through a yoke or to the waistline. Such plackets are usually faced with straight facings. A continuous bound placket is suitable for the opening at the side seam of the fitted dress. Methods of making plackets are given in Garment Construction, page 38.

Decorative Finishes.—Some dresses need a touch of trimming to add interest, but not all dresses need added decoration. The lines of the dress or the fabric may give all the interest needed. Bound buttonholes, attractive buttons, belt fastenings, decorative belts, flowers or lace trimmings are some of the touches which may be used to add interest. They should be very carefully planned or selected so that they will be in keeping with the dress in quality and weight and so the color will blend with that of the dress.

Buttons used on a dress opening usually call for buttonholes. Sewing on buttons for decoration, then using snap fasteners under the buttons, never makes as satisfactory or as attractive a closing as buttonholes would make.

Directions for making bound buttonholes and sewing on buttons and snaps are given in Garment Construction, page 46.

Order of Work.—Since some parts of a dress must be made before certain other parts, a girl will find it helpful and time saving to plan the order of her work. After thinking through the steps involved in making a dress, she makes a plan for her own dress, placing each step in its logical order. Checking through pages 5 to 19 in Garment Construction should help a girl follow the proper order. Her own plan is then written on page 23 of this circular.

Standards of Workmanship.—The care with which a girl handles her materials and does the stitching and pressing on her dress makes a great difference in the finished appearance of her dress. For this reason, materials should be handled as little and as carefully as possible. For instance, if a row of stitching has only a few stitches that are not straight, it is often best not to rip and re-stitch it. Hems should be carefully measured and basted, then ripping and re-stitching should not be necessary.

The finished appearance of the dress can usually be improved by pressing each seam before another one is joined to it, pressing collars and other finishes carefully before attaching them to the dress, and allowing plenty of time for finishing the dress properly (see Fig. 5). The Garment Construction bulletin contains many helpful suggestions which should help to improve any girl's standards of dress construction.

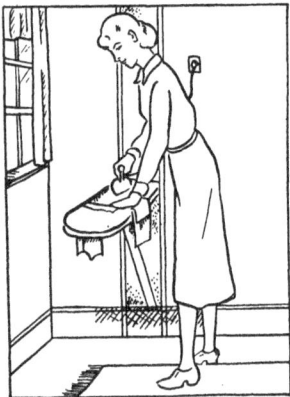

Fig. 5.—Press as you work.

The 4-H Club Girl Cares for Her Dress-up Dresses

A GIRL should be able to wash her dressy dress satisfactorily, provided the fabric was pre-shrunk, the design simple, and the dress well made (stitching firm and raw edges finished). Washing a dressy dress, however, requires careful and skillful handling.

Washing the Dressy Dress.—The suds should be prepared first by using about 1 tablespoon of mild soap flakes for each gallon of water. The flakes should be dissolved in a small amount of hot water, then enough of this solution added to a pan of cold water to make a lasting suds. The temperature for silk, rayon, and colored cotton fabrics should not be more than lukewarm, or 90°F., and may be less than lukewarm. At least two pans of suds should be prepared.

The dress should first be tested to make sure it is washable by washing a small sample. If the sample washes satisfactorily the dress should be shaken to remove surface dust, then examined for stains. Food stains, such as fruit and grease, are the most common ones found on dressy dresses. The fruit stains may be removed by stretching the stained part of the dress over a bowl and pouring boiling water upon the stain. The teakettle should be held a foot or more above the stain so the water strikes the spot with force. If boiling water will spoil the fabric the stain should be placed over a towel and sponged with cold water until it disappears. Grease spots and other stains which ordinarily wash out, should be outlined with white basting thread so they may be found easily during the washing process. If the dress does not need washing, carbon tetrachloride may be used to remove the grease spot. Bows or knots should be untied and buckles and perishable trimmings removed.

The dress should then be put through the two suds. This must be done as quickly as possible, squeezing the soapy water repeatedly through the fabric. All spots and soiled places should be given extra squeezing and care taken not to rub or twist the fabric.

When the dress is clean, it should be rinsed through two or three cold waters or until the last water shows no trace of soap. Unless the dress is unusually soiled, it should not be necessary to have it in the water longer than five minutes.

For cotton dresses a little cooked laundry starch may be added to the last rinse, while gum arabic will restore the newness to silk or rayon fabrics. Two teaspoons of powdered gum arabic should be added to one cup of hot water, stirred until dissolved, then cooled. All or part of this solution may be added to the last rinse water according to the stiffness desired. No specific directions can be given as to the exact amount to use, for some silks need more than others. A few trials will help to determine how much to use.

The water should be squeezed from the dress, never wrung out. For quick drying, the dress should be spread on one bath towel, a second towel inserted between the front and back of the dress, and a third towel spread on top. The towels should then be rolled so that the moisture is pressed from the dress into the towels. The dress should be removed at once and if there is any doubt as to color fastness, it should be shaken until dry enough to iron. If the color is fast the wrinkles should first be shaken out then the dress placed on a hanger and hung in the breeze until dry enough to iron.

Pressing the Dressy Dress.—Silk and rayon dresses should be pressed directly on the wrong side, using a moderate or cool iron and a wool padded ironing board. It is well to test the iron by trying it on a sample or seam edge before pressing the dress. With many silks a more lovely texture may be secured if the weight of the iron is not too great. Crepes should never be flattened in ironing. Care should be taken not to iron a crease in the sleeve. If it is necessary to replace plaits in the dress from the right side, a pressing cloth should be used.

Cotton dresses may be ironed on the right side unless there is a raised design on the fabric or a dull appearance is desired on the right side. Better results are often had if seams, hems, facings, and collars are first pressed on the wrong side and then on the right. A fairly hot iron, but not hot enough to scorch, may be used for cottons. The heat of the iron should be tested by trying it on a piece of the fabric before beginning to press. Seams, belts, pockets, collars, cuffs, and other finishes should be pressed neatly, and care taken not to iron wrinkles into the dress.

Protecting Dressy Dresses from Dust.—If the dressy dress is not worn often it should be placed on a padded dress hanger and hung in a garment bag or cover made especially to protect the dress from dust.

Any girl can easily make a cover for her dressy dress if she does not have one. Covers may be made from heavy muslin or gingham. The firmer the weave, the more protection the cover will give. Heavy paper makes a satisfactory cover for temporary use. When planning the size of the garment cover a girl should allow twice the length of her dress plus ⅓ yard. The finished width should be about 20 inches. When making the cover, the material should be folded so that one end is about 6 inches longer than the other. The folded end forms the bottom of the cover and the 6 inches forms a flap over the top opening. An eyelet should be made in the center of the top fold through which the hook of a dress hanger may be inserted. Garment covers opened down the side are easier to use but more difficult to make.

Shoulder covers are also used to protect dresses. They may be made of muslin or similar fabric. To make a shoulder cover, two thicknesses of material should be used and the cover cut the shape of the hanger across the top and 2 inches wider than the hanger. The sides and curved top should be seamed, and the lower edge, which is straight, may be bound or hemmed.

Repairing Dressy Dresses.—It may seem like an arduous task to learn how to repair dresses neatly, yet any girl who learns to do her mending skillfully and promptly will always feel well rewarded for her efforts.

As was stated before, small details such as a loose button, snap fastener, or ripped stitching may keep a girl from being completely tidy.

Ripped machine stitching should be re-stitched and broken hand stitches renewed as soon as they are noticed. Loose buttons and snap fasteners should be sewed on before they come off. See Garment Construction, bulletin 155.

Thin places often appear at the elbow or under the arm of a dress. Darning these places promptly will prolong the life of the garment.

A girl may be unfortunate enough to tear a large hole in her dress-up dress. In this case she will need to mend the tear with an overhand patch. The overhand patch, if well made, is very difficult to see, and that is a good quality for any patch. It may be used on cotton, silk, or wool material. The tear should be cut square or rectangular and on the up-and-down and crosswise threads of the fabric. To make an overhand patch, one should have a piece of fabric which matches the garment. The size and shape of this material will need to be such that the up-and-down threads as well as the design in the patch can be matched with the up-and-down threads and design in the dress, and still be large enough to cover and extend ½ inch beyond the edges of the hole.

The edges of the patch should be turned ¼ inch to the wrong side and basted before it is applied to the dress. When placing the patch on the garment, the center of the patch should be placed over the center of the hole with the wrong side of the patch against the right side of the garment. The two should then be basted together.

After the patch has been basted in place, the garment should be creased along the edge of the patch

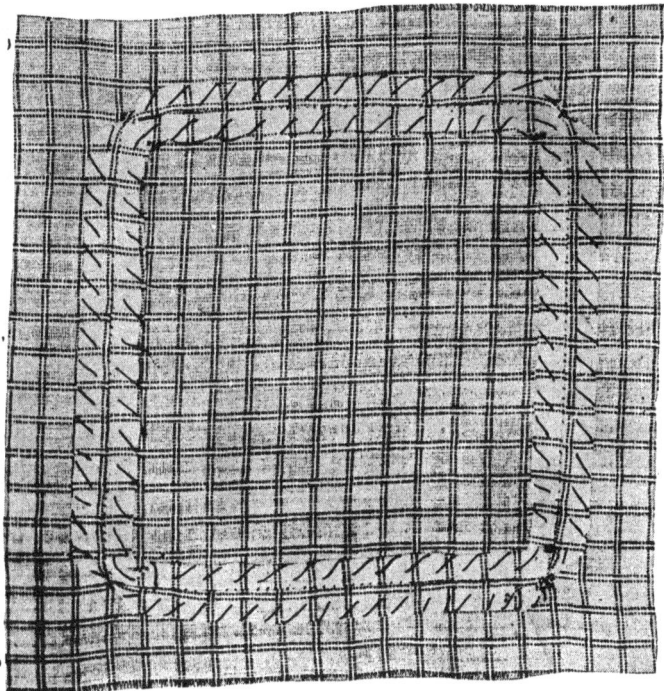

Fig. 6.—Overhand patch, wrong side.

and the two edges overhanded together with very small stitches placed close together. After the first side has been overhanded, the garment is turned and creased and the second side of the patch sewed to the dress, and so on until the whole patch is overhanded in place. Next, the garment is turned to the wrong side and the seams are pressed open, the corners of the patch cut away, and the corners of the garment cut diagonally so the seams will lie flat (see Fig. 6). If this patch is to wear well, one should overcast the raw edges of the seams on the wrong side. A well-made overhand patch is flat, neatly sewed, and almost invisible on the right side of the dress.

The overhand patch may be used on many garments. It is a good patch to use on silk and wool dresses and wool suits for men and boys. A girl who learns to patch well might make a specialty of mending the family's best clothes as well as helping with the weekly mending.

Statements and Questions About the 4-H Club Girl's Personal Appearance for Dress-up Occasions

Read "Dressing for Dress-up Occasions," pages 6 to 19 in this circular, and answer the following questions:

1. Name at least six factors important to making a good appearance.

a.. e. ....

b.. f...

c.. g..

d.. h..

2. Make out a good grooming program for yourself. List the different things that you will do at the different times, suggested below, and check (√) those needing special attention when grooming yourself for a dress-up party.

a. Every morning upon arising..................................

....

....

b. Every night before going to bed.................................

....

....

c. After each meal...

....

....

d. Whenever necessary during the day................................

....

....

e. Every week..

....

....

f. Less frequently...

....

....

3. Considering your complexion, do you need to use make-up for afternoon wear? Yes .... No................ (Check which.) Evening wear: Yes .... No ....

Give reasons for your answers..

....

....

4. What is your most becoming type of hairdress? ....

   Why? ....

   ....

   ....

5. How could you describe well-groomed hands? ....

   ....

   ....

6. Using a plumb line, check your posture, and record where plumb line passes:

	Through center	To right	To left of
Ear			
Shoulder			
Hip			
Knee			
Ankle			

7. According to the way you checked your posture above, is your posture

   excellent................ good................ fair................ poor................?

Care of Dress-up Dresses

Every 4-H club girl should aim to keep her dress-up dresses fresh and wearable. Read pages 17 to 19 in this circular, and complete the following sentences by putting in each blank a word which makes the statement correct.

1. When washing a garment by hand,

   a. Allow................ tablespoon of .... soapflakes to each gallon of soft water.

   b. Have the temperature of the water not more than ....

   c. .... the water through the fabric to remove the soil.

   d. .... water from garments, never twist them.

   e. Press silk and rayon fabrics directly on .... side, using a .... iron.

   f. Do not iron a .... down center of sleeves.

   g. Cotton fabrics may be pressed on either .... or .... side, with a .... iron.

2. How should the dressy dress be protected between wearings? ....

   ....

CHECKING YOURSELF AND YOUR EQUIPMENT

Before starting to sew, every 4-H club girl should check herself and her equipment. Read "Garment Construction," pages 3 and 4.

1. Make a list of the sewing supplies you keep in your sewing basket or box.

a.. d..

b.. e..

c.. f..

2. Do some machine stitching on a piece of material. Compare your stitching with the three samples shown here. Read the book that came with your sewing machine.

A—Both tensions correct.

B—Upper tension tighter than the lower.

C—Lower tension tighter than the upper.
—Copyright, S. M. Co.

Does your sample look like A, B, or C?..............................
If your sample looks like B or C, what adjustment can you make to either the top or bottom tensions to get the sample to look like A?..............................

....

....

....

3. Is the length of stitch in the stitching which you made on the sample of cloth suitable for the fabric you are using for your dress-up dress? ....
(Yes or No)
What size and color thread do you plan to use?.............................. If your machine is not making the correct length of stitch for your thread and fabric, adjust your machine so the stitch is satisfactory.

4. Check (√) your ability to do the following things. Which are you able to do well, and which ones do you need to know more about? Practice improving on these points as you select and make a dressy dress.

	Can Do Well	Should Practice
a. Check and alter a commercial pattern		
b. Select becoming colors		
c. Combine colors that look well together		
d. Fit a dress properly		
e. Select and make suitable finishes for dressy fabrics		
f. Keep self well groomed		
g. Keep dresses fresh and wearable		
h. Stand, sit and walk gracefully		

Planning a Becoming Dress

Choosing a Becoming Design.—Study "Dress Design," pages 10 to 12 in this circular, and answer the following:

1. How may the design for a dress-up dress vary from the design of a tailored dress? ....

....

2. What type of figure do you have? ....

3. What personality type are you? ....

4. Name three becoming features which you will look for when you are selecting the design for your dressy dress. ....

....

....

Choosing Becoming Colors.—Study pages 12 and 13 in this circular, and fill in the following:

1. What is your own personal coloring:

   Skin—Name the hue which best describes the color of your skin and tell whether you are light, medium, or dark. ....

   Lips and Cheeks—Name the hue which best describes the color of your lips and cheeks and tell whether they are bright, medium or pale.

   Lips .... Cheeks ....

   Eyes—Name the hue which best describes the color of your eyes and tell whether they are light, medium or dark. ....

   Hair—Describe the color of your hair, giving the hue, and tell whether it is light, medium or dark. ....

   Is there any additional color in your complexion that should be considered? .... If so, what is it? ....

2. List the colors you wear best. ....

....

Check (√) the one or ones you will use for your dress-up dress.

Fabrics for Dress-up Dresses

Before deciding on the fabric for your dress or dresses, read "Fabrics for the Dress-up Dress," pages 13 and 14 in this circular, and answer the following questions.

1. Check (√) the following words which describe the type of fabric you feel will be most becoming to you.

Plain............	Stiff..........	Light colors...........
Small scale print...........	Soft..........	Transparent..........
Large scale print...........	Bright colors..........	Non-transparent...........
Shiny..........	Soft colors..........	Others..........
Dull..........	Dark colors..........	....

23

2. Check(√) the following words which describe the type of fabric you feel would be most practical for you.

Cotton..........   Dry cleanable............   Light colors..........

Silk..........   Sheer ....   Medium colors...........

Rayon ....   Medium weight..........   Dark colors..........

Washable...........

3. Look in the stores or through a catalog and decide on three different materials which you like. Write the names of these materials in the blanks at top of table below. Before buying your fabric answer the questions listed below with "yes" or "no" for each fabric. Choose a fabric having all "Yes" answers.

Questions to Consider When Buying Fabrics	Name of Fabrics		
a. Can I afford this fabric?		•	
b. Is the price reasonable for the quality?			
c. Does the material have the appearance and feel of good quality?			
d. Is the design in the fabric pleasing?			
e. Is the design in the fabric becoming to me?			
f. Is the color of the fabric pleasing?			
g. Is the color of the fabric becoming to me?			
h. Will the fabric require more than reasonable care?			
i. Is it suited to the style garment I am making?			
j. Is the fabric suitable for me to work with considering my experience (not ravel easily, etc.)?			

MAKING YOUR DRESS

Before cutting out your dress answer the following questions. (Read "Garment Construction," pages 13 and 14, and pages 14 to 16 in this circular.)

1. Is there anything you need to do to your fabric before you cut out your dress?
.... If so, what? ....

....

2. Is there anything you need to do to your pattern before you cut out your dress?
.... What? ....

3. Name two things you will do in cutting out your dress to insure accurate workmanship. ....

....

....

4. Make a list of all the seams, finishes and hand stitches you will use on your dress. (See pages 14 and 16 of this circular.)

   a. ....   f. ....
   b. ....   g. ....
   c. ....   h. ....
   d. ....   i. ....
   e. ....   j. ....

5. Plan the order in which you will work to make your dress. See page 14, "Garment Construction," and page 16 of this circular. Try to follow your plan.

   a. ....   k. ....
   b. ....   l. ....
   c. ....   m. ....
   d. ....   n. ....
   e. ....   o. ....
   f. ....   p. ....
   g. ....   q. ....
   h. ....   r. ....
   i. ....   s. ....
   j. ....   t. ....

Care of Your Dress-up Dresses

1. Record of garments cared for. Fill in the blanks in the following table each time you wash, iron, or press a garment for yourself or another member of the family. For example:

June 20   *My afternoon dresses*   2   *cotton*   *washed and ironed*

Date	Name of Garment	No.	Kind of Fabric	Type of Care Given

2. Record of garments darned or mended. Fill in the blanks in the following table each time you darn or mend a garment for yourself or another member of the family. For example:

June 19   *My afternoon dress*   *overhand patch*   *1*

Date	Name of Garment	Kind of repair	No. of Repairs

Judging Your Dress

Judge your dress-up dress. The construction of your dress can be judged after each part is finished. The appearance cannot be scored until after the whole garment has been finished and tried on. When checking the construction of a dress ask yourself these questions about each of the finishes: is the method suitable? will the finish wear well? does the finish look neat on both the right and wrong sides? Consider your answers to these questions and give yourself one grade for each item listed. Grade only the things that apply to your dress. To figure the value of the check marks, multiply the number of check marks in each column by the figure at the top of the column. To arrive at the final score, add the total values of the check marks and divide by the number of points judged. 4=A, Excellent; 3=B, Good; 2=C, Average; 1=D, Unsatisfactory.

CONSTRUCTION	4	3	2	1	APPEARANCE	4	3	2	1
Seams					Becomingness to girl				
Underarm and shoulder					Of fabric				
Waistline and yoke					Of color				
					Of design				
Hems					Suitability to use				
					Of fabric				
Neckline finish					Of color				
					Of design				
Armscye finish					Fit of garment				
Plaits					Comfort				
					Appearance				
Belt					Style				
Belt loops or swing tacks					Individuality				
					Fashion				
Pockets					**TOTAL VALUE OF CHECK MARKS**				
Bindings					Appearance score				

CONSTRUCTION	4	3	2	1		4	3	2	1
Facings									
Plackets					POSTURE AND GROOMING OF GIRL				
Tucks					CONDITION OF DRESS				
Gathers					APPEARANCE SCORE (transfer)				
Darts					CONSTRUCTION SCORE (transfer)				
Sewing on buttons and snaps									
Attaching buckles, bows, etc.					**TOTAL VALUE OF CHECK MARKS**				
Other finishes					FINAL SCORE				
					FINAL GRADE (A, B, C, D)				
Total value of check marks					TOTAL COST OF DRESS, $				
Construction score					TOTAL TIME REQUIRED FOR MAKING				

Checking Yourself

Looking back over your activities in the project, which of the following do you think you do well, and which do you need more help with? Read over your own records, p. 27. They will help you know how to check (√) the following.

	Do well	Need more help with
Maintaining good posture		
Keeping self well groomed	•	
Keeping clothes repaired, clean and well pressed		
Choosing suitable and becoming dresses for dress-up wear		
Fitting dresses so they look well and are comfortable		
Feeling poised and self-confident at social functions		

Have you improved your sewing skills? .... How do you know?

....

....

△

What You Have Done in Your 4-H Club, In Your Home, and In Your Community

4-H CLUB ACTIVITIES

1. Number of 4-H club meetings attended...

2. Number of demonstrations given at meetings........................

3. Did your club do judging?..

   Ways in which you took part...

   ....

4. Ways in which you helped in the project work part of meetings:

   ....

   ....

   ....

   ....

5. Committees served on..

   ....

   ....

   ....

   ....

6. Offices held in club this year. (not required; number of offices is limited)............ ......

....

....

7. Ways in which you helped in recreation of the club...

....

....

....

....

8. Exhibiting: Did you wear your dress at the local judging?.................................

                                                          Yes or No

9. Type of educational exhibit your club planned and arranged for the county exhibit. ....

....

....

....

Ways in which you helped:...

....

....

....

10. In what county activities did you take part?..

....

....

11. What did your club do as its community service program?................................

....

....

....

Ways in which you helped...

....

....

....

12. Did your club have an individual health program?..

                                                 Yes or No

13. Did your club have a local achievement meeting?..

                                                 Yes or No

Ways in which you helped with the program of the meeting................................

....

....

....

1. Dresses Made.

Name of Fabric	Cost of Dress
Total number of dresses made:................................	Total cost of dresses: $................................

2. How did the making of this dress help you in your family life?................................

....

....

....

3. How did you improve your grooming practices?................................

....

....

4. How did you care for your clothing? (summarize):................................

.. ..

....

....

.. . .

5. How many times did you darn or mend your clothes?

....

. ...

6. If you were to have bought a dress ready made similar in quality and construction to the one you have made, how much would it have cost?................................

By making your dress how much did you save?................................

Homemaking Projects for 4-H Club Members

4-H homemaking projects include, in addition to clothing, foods and nutrition, home furnishings, home management, and projects for older girls, 15-20 years.

△

4-H Clothing Projects

1. Useful Articles for the Inexperienced 4-H Club Girl.
   The 4-H club girl makes at least three household or useful articles.
   Keeps records.

2. Useful articles for the experienced 4-H club girl.
   The 4-H club girl makes at least three useful articles or accessories to be worn.
   Keeps records.

3. The 4-H club girls' dresses for home and play.
   The 4-H club girl plans and makes at least one dress; mends and cares for her home and play dresses.
   Keeps records.

4. The 4-H club girls' dresses for school, business, sports, and street.
   The 4-H club girl plans and makes at least one dress; mends and cares for her dresses.
   Keeps records.

5. The 4-H club girls' dress-up dresses.
   The 4-H club girl plans and makes at least one dress; mends and cares for her dresses.
   Keeps records.

6. Undergarments for the 4-H club girl.
   The 4-H club girl plans and makes at least two undergarments, mends and cares for her undergarments.
   Keeps records.

△

Projects for the 4-H Club Girl 15-20 Years

1. The Older 4-H Club Girls' Complete Costume.
   The 4-H club girl plans and makes a complete costume for an occasion selected by the girl; makes the dress and undergarments; selects foundation garment; selects hose, shoes, and other accessories if needed to complete the costume.
   Keeps records.

2. When 4-H Club Members Entertain. (Hospitality)
   4-H Discussion Outlines on Personality Development for older girls are available.

Index